Quick & Easy
Potatoes

p

Contents

Introduction

Without doubt the potato is the most popular vegetable in the world. On average we eat 109 kg/242 lb per head per annum, which is not surprising as it is one of the most versatile and hardy crops. The potato, first discovered by the Spanish conquistadors in the Andes of Peru, can grow at a higher altitude and in colder climates than any other crop except barley. Moreover, it is said to produce more food per acre than any other northern food crop.

Treasure of the New World

Along with the silver and gold which returned from the New World, the potato, tomato and peppers — which belong to the same botanical family — were to make a huge impact on sixteenth-century Europe. Due to the wide variety of potatoes available, and the fact that it could be cooked in so many different ways, this vegetable became one of the most important food sources on the continent, with Russia, Poland and Germany being the highest consumers.

The vegetable also became famous for both its healing and nutritional properties. The Italians believed it could heal a wound if the cooked flesh was rubbed into the infected area. Although this has not withstood the test of time, the nutritional value of this tuber is indisputable. An average-sized potato weighing 100 g/4 oz contains 86 calories, is rich in

carbohydrate, vitamins B and C, and fibre, with a tiny amount of protein and some mineral salts (calcium, potassium, iron, and iodine).

The Variety

Potatoes are starchy tubers and all of them grow underground, several to one plant. The difference in shape, size and texture is enormous. The large Desirée can weigh 500 g/1 lb, while new season's new potatoes can weigh less than 15 g/1/2 oz. The skin-colour range is also vast, from cream through yellow, brown, pink, red, purple to black, while the skin texture can be smooth or netted. Each potato favours a different method of cooking, although there are also a few all-rounders. This and the variety in consistencies lends this vegetable to many uses.

Although there are thousands of different potatoes throughout the world, there are three main types of potato crop — first earlies, second earlies and main-crop. As the name suggests, the earlies are available first, usually from late May, and are referred to in Britain as 'new' potatoes. Main-crop potatoes can be harvested from September until the following June.

This book shows just how many different ways the potato can be prepared. From a natural thickener in soups and pastas, to the main ingredient in hearty main course dishes, each variety can be put to a multitude of different uses.

KEY	
	Simplicity level 1 – 3 (1 easiest, 3 slightly harder)
	Preparation time
	Cooking time

Choosing Potatoes

When choosing potatoes, always look for the freshest samples. Newly dug potatoes are preferable and to enjoy them at their best they should be eaten soon after purchase. When buying new potatoes their skin should rub away easily. The skin should look tight and smooth as if the vegetable is bursting with freshness. Main-crop potatoes should, in particular, be free of damage. Always avoid potatoes which are turning green or sprouting, as they have been exposed to too much light and their flavour will be bitter and they will have higher levels of the natural toxicants called glycoalkaloids. All potatoes should be stored in a cool, dark, airy place.

Selected Potato Varieties

There are an estimated 3,000 varieties of potato, but of these only about 100 are regularly grown, and only about 20 can be easily found in greengrocers and on supermarket shelves.

- Craig Royal Red: a main crop potato, ready in July, it is non-floury (non-mealy) and has a pink or red skin. A waxy potato, it is best for frying and boiling or using in salads.

- Cyprus New Potato: found in late winter and spring, it is best simply scrubbed and boiled. Not a good mashing potato.
- Desirée: a high-quality, pink-skinned floury (mealy) potato, good for baking, frying, boiling and mashing.
- Home Guard: generally the first of the new potatoes. It blackens easily and collapses on cooking, so it is best boiled lightly in its skin.
- Jersey Royal: a delicious new potato. It appears from May to October, but is at its peak in August. It has a flaky skin and firm yellow flesh.
- King Edward: a large potato which is creamy white, or sometimes yellow in colour. Ideal for all cooking methods, it is a very popular multi-purpose variety.
- Maris Piper: a medium-firm potato with creamy white flesh. It is good for boiling and frying.
- New Potatoes: these generally have a white flesh and grow quickly. They are dug up in early summer and are best scraped and boiled to use in salads or eaten with melted butter.
- Pentland Crown: a thin-skinned, creamy white potato which is at its best in late winter. It has a floury (mealy) texture, making it ideal for mashing and baking.
- Pentland Hawk: a firm, white-fleshed potato, which is suitable for all methods of cooking.
- Pink Fir Apple: this long, knobbly potato has pink flesh and a firm, waxy texture. Good in salads.
- White Sweet Potato: smaller than the yam, although interchangeable, it is yellow-fleshed with a drier texture. Best fried, boiled or cooked in a casserole, it is ideal with spices.
- Yam: a red sweet potato which is orange-fleshed. It is best mashed in cakes and soufflés or roasted.

Sweet Potato & Onion Soup

This simple recipe uses the sweet potato with its distinctive flavour and colour, combined with a hint of orange and coriander (cilantro).

NUTRITIONAL INFORMATION

Calories 320   Sugars 26g
Protein . . . . .7g   Fat 7g
Carbohydrate . . .62g   Saturates 1g

   15 MINS   30 MINS

SERVES 4

INGREDIENTS

2 tbsp vegetable oil

900 g/2 lb sweet potatoes, diced

1 carrot, diced

2 onions, sliced

2 garlic cloves, crushed

600 ml/1 pint/2½ cups vegetable stock

300 ml/½ pint/1¼ cups unsweetened
    orange juice

225 ml/8 fl oz/1 cup low-fat natural yogurt

2 tbsp chopped fresh coriander (cilantro)

salt and pepper

TO GARNISH

coriander (cilantro) sprigs

orange rind

1 Heat the vegetable oil in a large saucepan and add the diced sweet potatoes and carrot, sliced onions and garlic. Sauté the vegetables gently for 5 minutes, stirring constantly.

2 Pour in the vegetable stock and orange juice and bring them to the boil.

3 Reduce the heat to a simmer, cover the saucepan and cook the vegetables for 20 minutes or until the sweet potato and carrot cubes are tender.

4 Transfer the mixture to a food processor or blender in batches and process for 1 minute until puréed. Return the purée to the rinsed-out saucepan.

5 Stir in the natural yogurt and chopped coriander (cilantro) and season to taste.

6 Serve the soup in warm bowls and garnish with coriander (cilantro) sprigs and orange rind.

VARIATION

This soup can be chilled before serving, if preferred. If chilling it, stir the yogurt into the dish just before serving. Serve in chilled bowls.

Speedy Beetroot (Beet) Soup

Quick and easy to prepare in a microwave oven, this deep red soup of puréed beetroot (beets) and potatoes makes a stunning first course.

NUTRITIONAL INFORMATION

Calories 120   Sugars 11g
Protein ....4g   Fat 2g
Carbohydrate ...22g   Saturates 1g

 20 MINS   30 MINS

SERVES 6

INGREDIENTS

1 onion, chopped

350 g/12 oz potatoes, diced

1 small cooking apple, peeled,
   cored and grated

3 tbsp water

1 tsp cumin seeds

500 g/1 lb 2 oz cooked beetroot (beets),
   peeled and diced

1 bay leaf

pinch of dried thyme

1 tsp lemon juice

600 ml/1 pint/2½ cups hot vegetable stock

4 tbsp soured cream

salt and pepper

few dill sprigs, to garnish

1   Place the onion, potatoes, apple and water in a large bowl. Cover and cook on HIGH power for 10 minutes.

2   Stir in the cumin seeds and cook on HIGH power for 1 minute.

3   Stir in the beetroot (beets), bay leaf, thyme, lemon juice and hot vegetable stock. Cover and cook on HIGH power for 12 minutes, stirring halfway through the cooking time.

4   Leave to stand, uncovered, for 5 minutes. Remove and discard the bay leaf. Strain the vegetables and reserve the liquid. Process the vegetables with a little of the reserved liquid in a food processor or blender until they are smooth and creamy. Alternatively, either mash the vegetables with a potato masher or press them through a strainer with the back of a wooden spoon.

5   Pour the vegetable purée into a clean bowl with the reserved liquid and mix well. Season to taste. Cover and cook on HIGH power for 4–5 minutes, until the soup is piping hot.

6   Serve the soup in warmed bowls. Swirl 1 tablespoon of soured cream into each serving and garnish with a few sprigs of fresh dill.

Indian Potato & Pea Soup

A slightly hot and spicy Indian flavour is given to this soup with the use of garam masala, chilli, cumin and coriander (cilantro).

NUTRITIONAL INFORMATION

Calories 153   Sugars 6g
Protein ....6g   Fat 6g
Carbohydrate ...18g   Saturates 1g

 5 MINS   35 MINS

SERVES 4

INGREDIENTS

2 tbsp vegetable oil

225 g/8 oz floury (mealy) potatoes, diced

1 large onion, chopped

2 garlic cloves, crushed

1 tsp garam masala

1 tsp ground coriander

1 tsp ground cumin

900 ml/1½ pints/3¾ cups vegetable stock

1 red chilli, chopped

100 g/3½ oz frozen peas

4 tbsp low-fat natural yogurt

salt and pepper

chopped fresh coriander (cilantro), to garnish

1 Heat the vegetable oil in a large saucepan and add the diced potatoes, onion and garlic. Sauté gently for about 5 minutes, stirring constantly. Add the ground spices and cook for 1 minute, stirring all the time.

2 Stir in the vegetable stock and chopped red chilli and bring the mixture to the boil. Reduce the heat, cover the pan and simmer for 20 minutes.

3 Add the peas and cook for a further 5 minutes. Stir in the yogurt and season to taste.

4 Pour the soup into warmed bowls, garnish with the chopped fresh coriander (cilantro) and serve hot with warm bread.

COOK'S TIP

For slightly less heat, deseed the chilli before adding it to the soup. Always wash your hands after handling chillies as they contain volatile oils that can irritate the skin and make your eyes burn if you touch your face.

Broccoli & Potato Soup

This creamy soup has a delightful pale green colouring and rich flavour from the blend of tender broccoli and blue cheese.

NUTRITIONAL INFORMATION

Calories 452	Sugars 4g
Protein 14g	Fat 35g
Carbohydrate ...20g	Saturates 19g

 5-10 MINS 40 MINS

SERVES 4

INGREDIENTS

2 tbsp olive oil

2 potatoes, diced

1 onion, diced

225 g/8 oz broccoli florets

125 g/4½ oz blue cheese, crumbled

1 litre/1¾ pints/4½ cups vegetable stock

150 ml/¼ pint/⅔ cup double (heavy) cream

pinch of paprika

salt and pepper

1 Heat the oil in a large saucepan. Add the potatoes and onion. Sauté, stirring constantly, for 5 minutes.

2 Reserve a few broccoli florets for the garnish and add the remaining broccoli to the pan. Add the cheese and vegetable stock.

COOK'S TIP

This soup freezes very successfully. Follow the method described here up to step 4, and freeze the soup after it has been puréed. Add the cream and paprika just before serving. Garnish and serve.

3 Bring to the boil, then reduce the heat, cover the pan and simmer for 25 minutes, until the potatoes are tender.

4 Transfer the soup to a food processor or blender in batches and process until the mixture is smooth. Alternatively, press the vegetables through a strainer with the back of a wooden spoon.

5 Return the purée to a clean saucepan and stir in the double (heavy) cream and a pinch of paprika. Season to taste with salt and pepper.

6 Blanch the reserved broccoli florets in a little boiling water for about 2 minutes, then lift them out of the pan with a slotted spoon.

7 Pour the soup into warmed individual bowls and garnish with the broccoli florets and a sprinkling of paprika. Serve immediately.

Leek, Potato & Carrot Soup

A quick chunky soup, ideal for a snack or a quick lunch. The leftovers can be puréed to make one portion of creamed soup for the next day.

NUTRITIONAL INFORMATION

Calories 156	Sugars 7g
Protein 4g	Fat 6g
Carbohydrate ...22g	Saturates 0.7g

 10 MINS 25 MINS

SERVES 2

INGREDIENTS

1 leek, about 175 g/6 oz

1 tbsp sunflower oil

1 garlic clove, crushed

700 ml/1¼ pints/3 cups vegetable stock

1 bay leaf

¼ tsp ground cumin

175 g/6 oz/1 cup potatoes, diced

125 g/4½ oz/1 cup coarsely grated carrot

salt and pepper

chopped parsley, to garnish

PUREED SOUP

5–6 tbsp milk

1–2 tbsp double (heavy) cream, crème
fraîche or soured cream

1 Trim off and discard some of the coarse green part of the leek, then slice thinly and rinse thoroughly in cold water. Drain well.

2 Heat the sunflower oil in a heavy-based saucepan. Add the leek and garlic, and fry over a low heat for about 2–3 minutes, until soft, but barely coloured. Add the vegetable stock, bay leaf and cumin and season to taste with salt and pepper. Bring the mixture to the boil, stirring constantly.

3 Add the diced potato to the saucepan, cover and simmer over a low heat for 10–15 minutes until the potato is just tender, but not broken up.

4 Add the grated carrot and simmer for a further 2–3 minutes. Adjust the seasoning, discard the bay leaf and serve sprinkled liberally with chopped parsley.

5 To make a puréed soup, first process the leftovers (about half the original soup) in a blender or food processor or press through a strainer until smooth and then return to a clean saucepan with the milk. Bring to the boil and simmer for 2–3 minutes. Adjust the seasoning and stir in the cream or crème fraîche before serving sprinkled with chopped parsley.

Potato & Bean Pâté

This pâté is easy to prepare and may be stored in the refrigerator for up to two days. Serve with small toasts, Melba toast or crudités.

NUTRITIONAL INFORMATION

Calories	94	Sugars	........5g
Protein	........6g	Fat	..........1g
Carbohydrate	...17g	Saturates	.....0.2g

 5 MINS   10 MINS

SERVES 4

I N G R E D I E N T S

100 g/3½ oz floury (mealy) potatoes, diced

225 g/8 oz mixed canned beans, such as borlotti, flageolet and kidney beans, drained

1 garlic clove, crushed

2 tsp lime juice

1 tbsp chopped fresh coriander (cilantro)

2 tbsp low-fat natural yogurt

salt and pepper

chopped fresh coriander (cilantro), to garnish

1 Cook the potatoes in a saucepan of boiling water for 10 minutes until tender. Drain well and mash.

2 Transfer the potato to a food processor or blender and add the beans, garlic, lime juice and the fresh coriander (cilantro).

3 Season the mixture with salt and pepper and process for 1 minute to make a smooth purée. Alternatively, mix the beans with the potato, garlic, lime juice and coriander (cilantro) and mash.

4 Turn the purée into a bowl and add the yogurt. Mix well and season with salt and pepper to taste.

5 Spoon the pâté into a serving dish and garnish with the chopped coriander (cilantro). Serve at once or leave to chill.

COOK'S TIP

If you do not have a food processor or you would prefer to make a chunkier pâté, simply mash the ingredients with a fork.

Smoked Fish & Potato Pâté

This smoked fish pâté is given a tart fruity flavour by the gooseberries, which complement the fish perfectly.

NUTRITIONAL INFORMATION

Calories 418   Sugars 4g
Protein . . . . .18g   Fat 25g
Carbohydrate . . .32g   Saturates 6g

20 MINS   10 MINS

SERVES 4

I N G R E D I E N T S

650 g/1 lb 7 oz floury (mealy) potatoes, diced

300 g/10½ oz smoked mackerel, skinned and flaked

75 g/2¾ oz cooked gooseberries

2 tsp lemon juice

2 tbsp low-fat crème fraîche

1 tbsp capers

1 gherkin, chopped

1 tbsp chopped dill pickle

1 tbsp chopped fresh dill

salt and pepper

lemon wedges, to garnish

toast or warm crusty bread, to serve

1 Cook the diced potatoes in a saucepan of boiling water for 10 minutes until tender, then drain well.

2 Place the cooked potatoes in a food processor or blender.

3 Add the skinned and flaked smoked mackerel and process for 30 seconds until fairly smooth. Alternatively, place the ingredients in a bowl and mash with a fork.

4 Add the cooked gooseberries, lemon juice and crème fraîche to the fish and potato mixture. Blend for a further 10 -seconds or mash well.

5 Stir in the capers, chopped gherkin and dill pickle, and chopped fresh dill. Season well with salt and pepper.

6 Turn the fish pâté into a serving dish, garnish with lemon wedges and serve with slices of toast or warm crusty bread cut into chunks or slices.

COOK'S TIP

Use stewed, canned or bottled cooked gooseberries for convenience and to save time, or when fresh gooseberries are out of season.

Grilled (Broiled) Potatoes

This dish is ideal with grilled (broiled) or barbecued foods, as the potatoes themselves may be cooked by either method.

NUTRITIONAL INFORMATION

Calories 417   Sugars 1g
Protein . . . . .3g   Fat 37g
Carbohydrate . . .20g   Saturates 10g

 15 MINS   20 MINS

SERVES 4

I N G R E D I E N T S

450 g/1 lb potatoes, unpeeled and scrubbed

40 g/1½ oz/3 tbsp butter, melted

2 tbsp chopped thyme

paprika, for dusting

L I M E   M A Y O N N A I S E

150 ml/¼ pint/⅔ cup mayonnaise

2 tsp lime juice

finely grated rind of 1 lime

1 garlic clove, crushed

pinch of paprika

salt and pepper

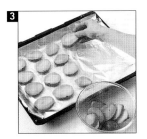

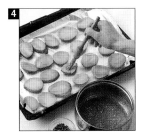

1 Cut the potatoes into 1 cm/½ inch thick slices.

2 Cook the potatoes in a saucepan of boiling water for 5–7 minutes – they should still be quite firm. Remove the potatoes with a slotted spoon and drain thoroughly.

3 Line a grill (broiler) pan with kitchen foil. Place the potato slices on top of the foil.

4 Brush the potatoes with the melted butter and sprinkle the chopped thyme on top. Season to taste with salt and pepper.

5 Cook the potatoes under a preheated grill (broiler) at medium heat for 10 minutes, turning once.

6 Meanwhile, make the lime mayonnaise. Thoroughly combine the mayonnaise, lime juice, lime rind, garlic, paprika and salt and pepper to taste in a small bowl.

7 Dust the hot potato slices with a little paprika and serve immediately with the lime mayonnaise.

COOK'S TIP

The lime mayonnaise may be spooned over the grilled (broiled) potatoes to coat them just before serving, if you prefer.

Potato & Mushroom Hash

This is a quick one-pan dish which is ideal for a quick snack. Packed with colour and flavour, you can add any other vegetable you have at hand.

NUTRITIONAL INFORMATION

Calories	378	Sugars	........14g
Protein	........18g	Fat	..........26g
Carbohydrate	...20g	Saturates	......7g

  10 MINS | 35 MINS

SERVES 4

INGREDIENTS

675 g/1½ lb potatoes, cubed

1 tbsp olive oil

2 garlic cloves, crushed

1 green (bell) pepper, cubed

1 yellow (bell) pepper, cubed

3 tomatoes, diced

75 g/2¾ oz/1 cup button mushrooms, halved

1 tbsp Worcester sauce

2 tbsp chopped basil

salt and pepper

fresh basil sprigs, to garnish

warm, crusty bread, to serve

1 Cook the potatoes in a saucepan of boiling salted water for 7–8 minutes. Drain well and reserve.

2 Heat the oil in a large, heavy-based frying pan (skillet) and cook the potatoes for 8–10 minutes, stirring until browned.

3 Add the garlic and (bell) peppers to the frying pan (skillet) and cook for 2–3 minutes.

4 Stir in the tomatoes and mushrooms and cook, stirring, for 5–6 minutes.

5 Stir in the Worcester sauce and basil and season well. Garnish with the fresh basil and serve with crusty bread.

COOK'S TIP

Most brands of Worcester sauce contain anchovies. If cooking for vegetarians, make sure you choose a vegetarian variety.

Thai Potato Crab Cakes

These small crab cakes are based on a traditional Thai recipe. They make a delicious snack when served with this sweet and sour cucumber sauce.

NUTRITIONAL INFORMATION

Calories ....254 Sugars 9g
Protein ....12g Fat 6g
Carbohydrate ...40g Saturates 1g

10 MINS   30 MINS

SERVES 4

INGREDIENTS

450 g/1 lb floury (mealy) potatoes, diced

175 g/6 oz white crab meat, drained if canned

4 spring onions (scallions), chopped

1 tsp light soy sauce

½ tsp sesame oil

1 tsp chopped lemon grass

1 tsp lime juice

3 tbsp plain (all-purpose) flour

2 tbsp vegetable oil

salt and pepper

SAUCE

4 tbsp finely chopped cucumber

2 tbsp clear honey

1 tbsp garlic wine vinegar

½ tsp light soy sauce

1 chopped red chilli

TO GARNISH

1 red chilli, sliced

cucumber slices

1 Cook the diced potatoes in a saucepan of boiling water for 10 minutes until cooked through. Drain well and mash.

2 Mix the crab meat into the potato with the spring onions (scallions), soy sauce, sesame oil, lemon grass, lime juice and flour. Season with salt and pepper.

3 Divide the potato mixture into 8 portions of equal size and shape them into small rounds, using floured hands.

4 Heat the oil in a wok or frying pan (skillet) and cook the cakes, 4 at a time, for 5-7 minutes, turning once. Keep warm and repeat with the remaining crab cakes.

5 Meanwhile, make the sauce. In a small serving bowl, mix the cucumber, honey, vinegar, soy sauce and chopped red chilli.

6 Garnish the cakes with the sliced red chilli and cucumber slices and serve with the sauce.

Chicken & Cheese Jackets

Use the breasts from a roasted chicken to make these delicious potatoes and serve as a light lunch or supper dish.

NUTRITIONAL INFORMATION

Calories 417   Sugars 4g
Protein . . . . .28g   Fat 10g
Carbohydrate . . .57g   Saturates 5g

  10 MINS 50 MINS

SERVES 4

I N G R E D I E N T S

4 large baking potatoes

225 g/8 oz cooked, boneless chicken breasts

4 spring onions (scallions)

250 g/9 oz/1 cup low-fat soft cheese or Quark

pepper

1 Scrub the potatoes and pat dry with absorbent kitchen paper (paper towels).

2 Prick the potatoes all over with a fork. Bake in a preheated oven, 200°C/400°F/Gas Mark 6, for about 50 minutes until tender, or cook in a microwave on HIGH/100% power for 12–15 minutes.

3 Using a sharp knife, dice the chicken and trim and thickly slice the spring onions (scallions). Place the chicken and spring onions (scallions) in a bowl.

4 Add the low-fat soft cheese or Quark to the chicken and spring onions (scallions) and stir well to combine.

5 Cut a cross through the top of each potato and pull slightly apart. Spoon the chicken filling into the potatoes and sprinkle with pepper.

6 Serve the chicken and cheese jackets immediately with coleslaw, green salad or a mixed salad.

COOK'S TIP

Look for Quark in the chilled section. It is a low-fat, white, fresh curd cheese made from cow's milk with a delicate, slightly sour flavour.

Potatoes en Papillotes

New potatoes are perfect for this recipe. The potatoes and vegetables are wrapped in greaseproof (waxed) paper, sealed and steamed in the oven.

NUTRITIONAL INFORMATION

Calories	85	Sugars	........4g
Protein	........2g	Fat	........0.5g
Carbohydrate	...15g	Saturates	.....0.1g

 10 MINS   35 MINS

SERVES 4

INGREDIENTS

16 small new potatoes

1 carrot, cut into matchstick strips

1 fennel bulb, sliced

75 g/2¾ oz French (green) beans

1 yellow (bell) pepper, cut into strips

16 tbsp dry white wine

4 rosemary sprigs

salt and pepper

rosemary sprigs, to garnish

1 Cut 4 squares of greaseproof (waxed) paper measuring about 25 cm/10 inches in size.

2 Divide the vegetables equally between the 4 paper squares, placing them in the centre.

3 Bring the edges of the paper together and scrunch them together to encase the vegetables, leaving the top open.

4 Place the parcels in a shallow roasting tin (pan) and spoon 4 tablespoons of white wine into each parcel. Add a rosemary sprig and season.

5 Fold the top of each parcel over to seal it. Cook in a preheated oven, 190°C/375°F/Gas Mark 5, for 30-35 minutes or until the vegetables are tender.

6 Transfer the sealed parcels to 4 individual serving plates and garnish with rosemary sprigs.

7 Open the parcels at the table in order for the full aroma of the vegetables to be appreciated.

COOK'S TIP

If small new potatoes are unavailable, use larger potatoes which have been halved or quartered to ensure that they cook through in the specified cooking time.

Potato Omelette

This quick chunky omelette has pieces of potato cooked into the egg mixture and is then filled with feta cheese and spinach.

NUTRITIONAL INFORMATION

Calories	564	Sugars	.........6g
Protein	........30g	Fat	.........39g
Carbohydrate	...25g	Saturates	......19g

20 MINS   25-30 MINS

SERVES 4

I N G R E D I E N T S

75 g/2¾ oz/⅓ cup butter

6 waxy potatoes, diced

3 garlic cloves, crushed

1 tsp paprika

2 tomatoes, peeled, seeded and diced

12 eggs

pepper

F I L L I N G

225 g/8 oz baby spinach

1 tsp fennel seeds

125 g/4½ oz feta cheese, diced

4 tbsp natural (unsweetened) yogurt

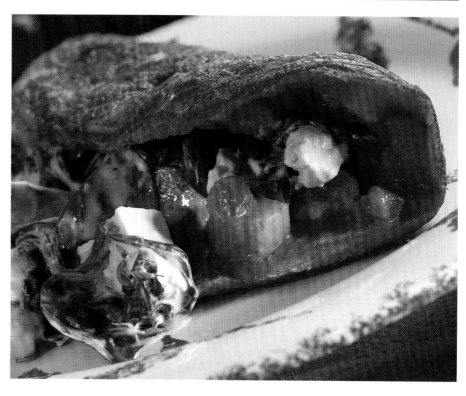

1 Heat 25 g/1 oz/2 tbsp of the butter in a frying pan (skillet) and cook the potatoes over a low heat, stirring constantly, for 7-10 minutes until golden. Transfer to a bowl.

2 Add the garlic, paprika and tomatoes to the pan and cook for a further 2 minutes.

3 Whisk the eggs together and season with pepper. Pour the eggs into the potatoes and mix well.

4 Cook the spinach in boiling water for 1 minute, until just wilted. Drain and refresh under cold running water. Pat dry with kitchen paper (paper towels). Stir in the fennel seeds, feta cheese and yogurt.

5 Heat a quarter of the remaining butter in a 15 cm/6 inch omelette pan. Ladle a quarter of the egg and potato mixture into the pan. Cook, turning once, for 2 minutes, until set.

6 Transfer the omelette to a serving plate. Spoon a quarter of the spinach mixture on to one half of the omelette, then fold the omelette in half over the filling. Repeat to make 4 omelettes.

VARIATION

Use any other cheese, such as blue cheese, instead of the feta and blanched broccoli in place of the baby spinach, if you prefer.

Cheese & Potato Slices

This recipe takes a while to prepare but it is well worth the effort. The golden potato slices coated in breadcrumbs and cheese are delicious.

NUTRITIONAL INFORMATION

Calories 560   Sugars 3g
Protein . . . . .19g   Fat 31g
Carbohydrate . . .55g   Saturates 7g

10 MINS   40 MINS

SERVES 4

INGREDIENTS

3 large waxy potatoes, unpeeled and
  thickly sliced

75 g/2½ oz/1 cup fresh white breadcrumbs

40 g/1½ oz/½ cup grated Parmesan
  cheese

1½ tsp chilli powder

2 eggs, beaten

oil, for deep frying

chilli powder, for dusting (optional)

1 Cook the sliced potatoes in a saucepan of boiling water for about 10-15 minutes, or until the potatoes are just tender. Drain thoroughly.

2 Mix the breadcrumbs, cheese and chilli powder together in a bowl, then transfer to a shallow dish. Pour the beaten eggs into a separate shallow dish.

3 Dip the potato slices first in egg and then roll them in the breadcrumbs to coat completely.

4 Heat the oil in a large saucepan or deep-fryer to 180°C/350°F or until a cube of bread browns in 30 seconds. Cook the cheese and potato slices, in several batches, for 4–5 minutes or until a golden brown colour.

5 Remove the cheese and potato slices from the oil with a slotted spoon and drain thoroughly on kitchen paper (paper towels). Keep the cheese and potato slices warm while you cook the remaining batches.

6 Transfer the cheese and potato slices to warm individual serving plates. Dust lightly with chilli powder, if using, and serve immediately.

COOK'S TIP

The cheese and potato slices may be coated in the breadcrumb mixture in advance and then stored in the refrigerator until ready to use.

Potato Mushroom Cakes

These cakes will be loved by vegetarians and meat-eaters alike. Packed with creamy potato and as wide a variety of mushrooms as possible.

NUTRITIONAL INFORMATION

Calories 298   Sugars 0.8g
Protein . . . . .5g   Fat 22g
Carbohydrate . . .22g   Saturates 5g

🍲 20 MINS   🕙 25 MINS

SERVES 4

I N G R E D I E N T S

500 g/1 lb 2 oz floury (mealy) potatoes,
    diced

25 g/1 oz/2 tbsp butter

175 g/6 oz mixed mushrooms, chopped

2 garlic cloves, crushed

1 small egg, beaten

1 tbsp chopped fresh chives, plus extra
    to garnish

flour, for dusting

oil, for frying

salt and pepper

1 Cook the potatoes in a pan of lightly salted boiling water for 10 minutes, or until cooked through

2 Drain the potatoes well, mash with a potato masher or fork and set aside.

3 Meanwhile, melt the butter in a frying pan (skillet). Add the mushrooms and garlic and cook, stirring constantly, for 5 minutes. Drain well.

4 Stir the mushrooms and garlic into the potato, together with the beaten egg and chives.

5 Divide the mixture equally into 4 portions and shape them into round cakes. Toss them in the flour until the outsides of the cakes are completely coated.

6 Heat the oil in a frying pan (skillet). Add the potato cakes and fry over a medium heat for 10 minutes until they are golden brown, turning them over halfway through. Serve the cakes at once, with a simple crisp salad.

COOK'S TIP

Prepare the cakes in advance, cover and leave to chill in the refrigerator for up to 24 hours, if you wish.

Potato Fritters with Relish

These are incredibly simple to make and sure to be popular served as a tempting snack or as an accompaniment to almost any Indian meal.

NUTRITIONAL INFORMATION

Calories 294   Sugars 4g
Protein . . . . .4g   Fat 24g
Carbohydrate . . .18g   Saturates 3g

40 MINS   15 MINS

SERVES 8

I N G R E D I E N T S

60 g/2 oz/½ cup plain wholemeal (whole
  wheat) flour

½ tsp ground coriander

½ tsp cumin seeds

¼ tsp chilli powder

½ tsp ground turmeric

¼ tsp salt

1 egg

3 tbsp milk

350 g/12 oz potatoes, peeled

1-2 garlic cloves, crushed

4 spring onions (scallions), chopped

60 g/2 oz corn kernels

vegetable oil, for shallow frying

O N I O N & T O M A T O
R E L I S H

1 onion, peeled

225 g/8 oz tomatoes

2 tbsp chopped coriander (cilantro)

2 tbsp chopped mint

2 tbsp lemon juice

½ tsp roasted cumin seeds

¼ tsp salt

pinch of cayenne pepper

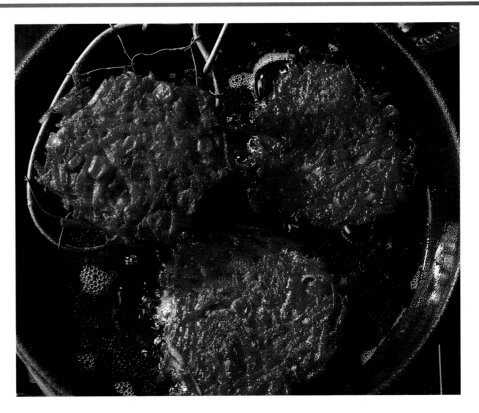

1 First make the relish. Cut the onion and tomatoes into small dice and place in a bowl with the remaining ingredients. Mix together well and leave to stand for at least 15 minutes before serving to allow time for the flavours to blend.

2 Place the flour in a bowl, stir in the spices and salt and make a well in the centre. Add the egg and milk and mix to form a fairly thick batter.

3 Coarsely grate the potatoes, place in a sieve and rinse well under cold running water. Drain and squeeze dry, then stir into the batter with the garlic, spring onions (scallions) and corn.

4 Heat about 5 mm/¼ inches vegetable oil in a large frying pan and add a few tablespoonfuls of the mixture at a time, flattening each one to form a thin cake. Fry over a low heat, turning frequently, for 2-3 minutes, or until golden brown and cooked through.

5 Drain on kitchen paper (paper towels) and keep hot while frying the remaining mixture in the same way. Serve hot with onion and tomato relish.

Creamy Mushroom & Potato

These oven-baked mushrooms are covered with a creamy potato and mushroom filling topped with melted cheese.

NUTRITIONAL INFORMATION

Calories	214	Sugars	. . . . .1g
Protein	. . . . .5g	Fat	. . . . .17g
Carbohydrate	. . . .11g	Saturates	. . . . . .11g

   40 MINS   40 MINS

SERVES 4

I N G R E D I E N T S

25 g/1 oz dried ceps

225 g/8 oz floury (mealy) potatoes, diced

25 g/1 oz/2 tbsp butter, melted

4 tbsp double (heavy) cream

2 tbsp chopped fresh chives

25 g/1 oz/¼ cup grated Emmental cheese

8 large open-capped mushrooms

150 ml/¼ pint/⅔cup vegetable stock

salt and pepper

fresh chives, to garnish

1 Place the dried ceps in a small bowl. Add sufficient boiling water to cover and set aside to soak for 20 minutes.

2 Meanwhile, cook the potatoes in a medium saucepan of lightly salted boiling water for 10 minutes, until cooked through and tender. Drain well and mash until smooth.

3 Drain the soaked ceps and then chop them finely. Mix them into the mashed potato.

4 Thoroughly blend the butter, cream and chives together and pour the mixture into the ceps and potato mixture, mixing well. Season to taste with salt and pepper.

5 Remove the stalks from the open-capped mushrooms. Chop the stalks and stir them into the potato mixture. Spoon the mixture into the open-capped mushrooms and sprinkle the cheese over the top.

6 Arrange the filled mushrooms in a shallow ovenproof dish and pour in the vegetable stock.

7 Cover the dish and cook in a preheated oven, 220°C/ 425°F/Gas Mark 7, for 20 minutes. Remove the lid and cook for 5 minutes until golden.

8 Garnish the mushrooms with fresh chives and serve at once.

VARIATION

Use fresh mushrooms instead of the dried ceps, if preferred, and stir a mixture of chopped nuts into the mushroom stuffing mixture for extra crunch.

Crispy Potato Skins

Potato skins are always a favourite. Prepare the skins in advance and warm through before serving with the salad fillings.

NUTRITIONAL INFORMATION

Calories ....332 Sugars 18g
Protein ....8g Fat 14g
Carbohydrate ...47g Saturates 5g

30 MINS   1HR 10 MINS

SERVES 4

I N G R E D I E N T S

4 large baking potatoes

2 tbsp vegetable oil

4 tsp salt

snipped chives, to garnish

150 ml/¼ pint/⅔ cup soured cream
  and 2 tbsp chopped chives, to serve

B E A N S P R O U T   S A L A D

50 g/1¾ oz/½ cup beansprouts

1 celery stick, sliced

1 orange, peeled and segmented

1 red eating apple, chopped

½ red (bell) pepper, seeded and chopped

1 tbsp chopped parsley

1 tbsp light soy sauce

1 tbsp clear honey

1 small garlic clove, crushed

B E A N   F I L L I N G

100 g/3½ oz/1½ cups canned, mixed
  beans, drained

1 onion, halved and sliced

1 tomato, chopped

2 spring onions (scallions), chopped

2 tsp lemon juice

salt and pepper

1 Scrub the potatoes and put on a baking sheet (cookie sheet). Prick the potatoes all over with a fork and rub the oil and salt into the skins.

2 Cook in a preheated oven, 200°C/400°F/Gas Mark 6 for 1 hour or until soft and cooked through.

3 Cut the potatoes in half lengthways and scoop out the flesh, leaving a 1 cm/½ inch thick shell. Put the shells, skin side uppermost, in the oven for 10 minutes, until crisp.

4 Mix the ingredients for the beansprout salad in a bowl, tossing in the soy sauce, honey and garlic to coat.

5 Mix the ingredients for the bean filling in a separate bowl.

6 Mix the soured cream and chives in another bowl.

7 Serve the potato skins hot, with the two salad fillings, garnished with snipped chives, and the soured cream and chive sauce.

Hash Browns

Hash Browns are a popular American recipe of fried potato squares, often served as brunch. This recipe includes extra vegetables.

NUTRITIONAL INFORMATION

Calories 339   Sugars 9g
Protein . . . . .10g   Fat 21g
Carbohydrate . . .29g   Saturates 7g

 20 MINS   45 MINS

SERVES 4

I N G R E D I E N T S

500 g/1 lb 2 oz waxy potatoes

1 carrot, diced

1 celery stick, diced

60 g/2 oz button mushrooms, diced

1 onion, diced

2 garlic cloves, crushed

25 g/1 oz/¼ cup frozen
   peas, thawed

60 g/2 oz/⅔ cup grated
   Parmesan cheese

4 tbsp vegetable oil

25 g/1 oz/2 tbsp butter

salt and pepper

S A U C E

300 ml/½ pint/1¼ cups passata (sieved
   tomatoes)

2 tbsp chopped fresh coriander (cilantro)

1 tbsp vegetarian Worcestershire sauce

½ tsp chilli powder

2 tsp brown sugar

2 tsp American mustard

75 ml/3 fl oz/⅓ cup vegetable stock

1 Cook the potatoes in a saucepan of lightly salted boiling water for 10 minutes. Drain and leave to cool. Meanwhile, cook the carrot in lightly salted boiling water for 5 minutes.

2 Set the potato aside to cool. When cool enough to handle, grate it with a coarse grater.

3 Drain the carrot and add it to the grated potato, together with the celery, mushrooms, onion, garlic, peas and cheese. Season to taste with salt and pepper.

4 Put all of the sauce ingredients in a small saucepan and bring to the boil. Reduce the heat to low and simmer for 15 minutes.

5 Divide the potato mixture into 8 portions of equal size and shape into flattened rectangles with your hands.

6 Heat the oil and butter in a frying pan (skillet) and cook the hash browns over a low heat for 4-5 minutes on each side, until crisp and golden brown.

7 Transfer the hash browns to a serving plate and serve immediately with the tomato sauce.

Carrot & Potato Soufflé

Hot soufflés have a reputation for being difficult to make, but this one is both simple and impressive. Make sure you serve it as soon as it is ready.

NUTRITIONAL INFORMATION

Calories 294	Sugars 6g	
Protein 10g	Fat 9g	
Carbohydrate ...46g	Saturates 4g	

🥔 1¼ HOURS   🕐 40 MINS

SERVES 4

I N G R E D I E N T S

25 g/1 oz/2 tbsp butter, melted

4 tbsp fresh wholemeal (whole wheat)
   breadcrumbs

675 g/1½ lb floury (mealy) potatoes, baked
   in their skins

2 carrots, grated

2 eggs, separated

2 tbsp orange juice

¼ tsp grated nutmeg

salt and pepper

carrot curls, to garnish

1 Brush the inside of a 900 ml/
1½ pint/3¾ cup soufflé dish with
butter. Sprinkle three-quarters of the
breadcrumbs over the base and sides.

2 Cut the baked potatoes in half and
scoop the flesh into a mixing bowl.

3 Add the carrot, egg yolks, orange juice
and nutmeg to the potato flesh.
Season to taste with salt and pepper.

4 In a separate bowl, whisk the egg
whites until soft peaks form, then
gently fold into the potato mixture with a
metal spoon until well incorporated.

5 Gently spoon the potato and carrot
mixture into the prepared soufflé dish.
Sprinkle the remaining breadcrumbs over
the top of the mixture.

6 Cook in a preheated oven, 200°C/
400°F/Gas Mark 6, for 40 minutes,
until risen and golden. Do not open the
oven door during the cooking time,
otherwise the soufflé will sink. Serve at
once, garnished with carrot curls.

COOK'S TIP

To bake the potatoes, prick
the skins and cook in a preheated oven, 190°C/375°F/Gas
Mark 5, for about 1 hour.

Spicy Potato Fries

These home-made chips (fries) are flavoured with spices and cooked in the oven. Serve with Lime Mayonnaise (see page 13).

NUTRITIONAL INFORMATION

Calories 328   Sugars 2g
Protein . . . . .5g   Fat 11g
Carbohydrate . . .56g   Saturates 7g

35 MINS   40 MINS

SERVES 4

I N G R E D I E N T S

4 large waxy potatoes

2 sweet potatoes

50 g/1¾ oz/4 tbsp butter, melted

½ tsp chilli powder

1 tsp garam masala

salt

1 Cut the potatoes and sweet potatoes into slices about 1 cm/½ inch thick, then cut them into chip (fries) shapes.

2 Place the potatoes in a large bowl of cold salted water. Set aside to soak for 20 minutes.

3 Remove the potato slices with a slotted spoon and drain thoroughly. Pat with kitchen paper (paper towels) until completely dry.

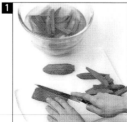

COOK'S TIP

Rinsing the potatoes in cold water before cooking removes the starch, thus preventing them from sticking together. Soaking the potatoes in a bowl of cold salted water actually makes the cooked chips (fries) crisper.

4 Pour the melted butter on to a baking tray (cookie sheet). Transfer the potato slices to the baking tray (cookie sheet).

5 Sprinkle with the chilli powder and garam masala, turning the potato slices to coat them with the mixture.

6 Cook the chips in a preheated oven, 200°C/400°F/Gas Mark 6, turning frequently, for 40 minutes, until browned and cooked through.

7 Drain the chips on kitchen paper (paper towels) to remove the excess oil and serve at once.

Potato Fritters

Chunks of cooked potato are coated first in Parmesan cheese, then in a light batter before being fried until golden for a delicious hot snack.

NUTRITIONAL INFORMATION

Calories	599	Sugars	........9g
Protein	........22g	Fat	..........39g
Carbohydrate	...42g	Saturates	......13g

🥔 20 MINS   🕐 20-25 MINS

SERVES 4

I N G R E D I E N T S

500 g/1 lb 2 oz waxy potatoes, cut into

large cubes

125 g/4½ oz/1¼ cups grated

Parmesan cheese

oil, for deep-frying

S A U C E

25 g/1 oz/2 tbsp butter

1 onion, halved and sliced

2 garlic cloves, crushed

25 g/1 oz/¼ cup plain (all-

purpose) flour

300 ml/½ pint/1¼ cups milk

1 tbsp chopped parsley

B A T T E R

50 g/1¾ oz/½ cup plain (all-purpose) flour

1 small egg

150 ml/¼ pint/⅔ cup milk

1 To make the sauce, melt the butter in a saucepan and cook the sliced onion and garlic over a low heat, stirring frequently, for 2-3 minutes. Add the flour and cook, stirring constantly, for 1 minute.

2 Remove from the heat and stir in the milk and parsley. Return to the heat and bring to the boil. Keep warm.

3 Meanwhile, cook the cubed potatoes in a saucepan of boiling water for 5-10 minutes, until just firm. Do not overcook or they will fall apart.

4 Drain the potatoes and toss them in the Parmesan cheese. If the potatoes are still slightly wet, the cheese sticks to them and coats them well.

5 To make the batter, place the flour in a mixing bowl and gradually beat in the egg and milk until smooth. Dip the potato cubes into the batter to coat them.

6 In a large saucepan or deep-fryer, heat the oil to 180°C/350°F or until a cube of bread browns in 30 seconds. Add the fritters and cook for 3-4 minutes, or until golden.

7 Remove the fritters with a slotted spoon and drain well. Transfer them to a warm serving bowl and serve immediately with the garlic sauce.

Potatoes Lyonnaise

In this classic French recipe, sliced potatoes are cooked with onions to make a delicious accompaniment to a main meal.

NUTRITIONAL INFORMATION

Calories . . . . . . .277 Sugars 4g
Protein . . . . .5g Fat 12g
Carbohydrate . . .40g Saturates 4g

 10 MINS   25 MINS

SERVES 6

I N G R E D I E N T S

1.25 kg/2 lb 12 oz potatoes

4 tbsp olive oil

25 g/1 oz/2 tbsp butter

2 onions, sliced

2–3 garlic cloves, crushed (optional)

salt and pepper

chopped parsley, to garnish

1 Slice the potatoes into 5 mm/¼ inch slices. Put in a large saucepan of lightly salted water and bring to the boil. Cover and simmer gently for about 10–12 minutes, until just tender. Avoid boiling too rapidly or the potatoes will break up and lose their shape. When cooked, drain well.

COOK'S TIP

If the potatoes blacken slightly as they are boiling, add a spoonful of lemon juice to the cooking water.

2 While the potatoes are cooking, heat the oil and butter in a very large frying pan (skillet). Add the onions and garlic, if using, and fry over a medium heat, stirring frequently, until the onions are softened.

3 Add the cooked potato slices to the frying pan (skillet) and cook with the onions, carefully stirring occasionally, for about 5–8 minutes until the potatoes are well browned.

4 Season to taste with salt and pepper. Sprinkle over the chopped parsley to serve. If wished, transfer the potatoes and onions to a large ovenproof dish and keep warm in a low oven until ready to serve.

Spiced Potatoes & Spinach

This is a classic Indian accompaniment for many different curries or plainer main vegetable dishes. It is very quick to cook.

NUTRITIONAL INFORMATION

Calories 176	Sugars 4g	
Protein 6g	Fat 9g	
Carbohydrate ...18g	Saturates 1g	

  10 MINS   20-25 MINS

SERVES 4

I N G R E D I E N T S

3 tbsp vegetable oil

1 red onion, sliced

2 garlic cloves, crushed

½ tsp chilli powder

2 tsp ground coriander

1 tsp ground cumin

150 ml/¼ pint/⅔ cup vegetable stock

300 g/10½ oz potatoes, diced

500 g/1 lb 2 oz baby spinach

1 red chilli, sliced

salt and pepper

1 Heat the oil in a heavy-based frying pan (skillet). Add the onion and garlic and sauté over a medium heat, stirring occasionally, for 2–3 minutes.

2 Stir in the chilli powder, ground coriander and cumin and cook, stirring constantly, for a further 30 seconds.

3 Add the vegetable stock, diced potatoes and spinach and bring to the boil. Reduce the heat, cover the frying pan (skillet) and simmer for about 10 minutes, or until the potatoes are cooked through and tender.

4 Uncover, season to taste with salt and pepper, add the chilli and cook for a further 2–3 minutes. Transfer to a warmed serving dish and serve immediately.

COOK'S TIP

Besides adding extra colour to a dish, red onions have a sweeter, less pungent flavour than other varieties.

Potato & Mushroom Bake

Use any mixture of mushrooms for this creamy layered bake. It can be served straight from the dish in which it is cooked.

NUTRITIONAL INFORMATION

Calories	304	Sugars	.........2g
Protein	.........4g	Fat	..........24g
Carbohydrate	...20g	Saturates	......15g

15 MINS   1 HOUR

SERVES 4

INGREDIENTS

25 g/1 oz/2 tbsp butter

500 g/1 lb 2 oz waxy potatoes, thinly sliced

150 g/5½ oz/2 cups sliced
   mixed mushrooms

1 tbsp chopped rosemary

4 tbsp chopped chives

2 garlic cloves, crushed

150 ml/¼ pint/⅔cup double (heavy) cream

salt and pepper

snipped chives, to garnish

1 Grease a shallow round ovenproof dish with butter.

2 Parboil the sliced potatoes in a saucepan of boiling water for 10 minutes. Drain well. Layer a quarter of the potatoes in the base of the dish.

3 Arrange one-quarter of the mushrooms on top of the potatoes and sprinkle with one-quarter of the rosemary, chives and garlic. Continue making layers in the same order, finishing with a layer of potatoes on top.

4 Pour the cream over the top of the potatoes. Season to taste with salt and pepper.

5 Cook in a preheated oven, 190°C/ 375°F/Gas Mark 5, for about 45 minutes, or until the bake is golden brown and piping hot.

6 Garnish with snipped chives and serve at once straight from the dish.

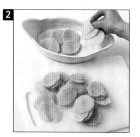  

COOK'S TIP

For a special occasion, the bake may be made in a lined cake tin (pan) and then turned out to serve.

Casseroled Potatoes

This potato dish is cooked in the oven with leeks and wine. It is very quick and simple to make.

NUTRITIONAL INFORMATION

Calories 187   Sugars 2g
Protein . . . . .4g   Fat 3g
Carbohydrate . . .31g   Saturates 2g

🥔 10 MINS   🕐 50 MINS

SERVES 4

I N G R E D I E N T S

675 g/1½ lb waxy potatoes, cut into chunks

15 g/½ oz/1 tbsp butter

2 leeks, sliced

150 ml/¼ pint/⅔ cup dry white wine

150 ml/¼ pint/⅔ cup vegetable stock

1 tbsp lemon juice

2 tbsp chopped mixed fresh herbs

salt and pepper

T O   G A R N I S H

grated lemon rind

mixed fresh herbs (optional)

1 Cook the potato chunks in a saucepan of boiling water for 5 minutes. Drain thoroughly.

2 Meanwhile, melt the butter in a frying pan (skillet) and sauté the leeks for 5 minutes or until they have softened.

3 Spoon the partly cooked potatoes and leeks into an ovenproof dish.

4 In a measuring jug, mix together the wine, vegetable stock, lemon juice and chopped mixed herbs. Season to taste with salt and pepper, then pour the mixture over the potatoes.

5 Cook in a preheated oven, 190°C/375°F/Gas Mark 5, for 35 minutes or until the potatoes are tender.

6 Garnish the potato casserole with lemon rind and fresh herbs (if using) and serve as an accompaniment to meat casseroles or roast meat.

COOK'S TIP

Cover the ovenproof dish halfway through cooking if the leeks start to brown on the top.

Potato & Spinach Triangles

These small pasties are made with crisp filo pastry and filled with a tasty spinach and potato mixture flavoured with chilli and tomato.

NUTRITIONAL INFORMATION

Calories 514   Sugars 4g
Protein . . . . .9g   Fat 37g
Carbohydrate . . .37g   Saturates 8g

 25 MINS   🕐 35 MINS

SERVES 4

INGREDIENTS

25 g/1 oz/2 tbsp butter, melted, plus extra
   for greasing

225 g/8 oz waxy potatoes, finely diced

500 g/1 lb 2 oz baby spinach

1 tomato, seeded and chopped

¼ tsp chilli powder

½ tsp lemon juice

225 g/8 oz filo pastry, thawed if frozen

salt and pepper

crisp salad, to serve

LEMON MAYONNAISE

150 ml/¼ pint/⅔ cup mayonnaise

2 tsp lemon juice

rind of 1 lemon

1 Lightly grease a baking tray (cookie sheet) with a little butter.

2 Cook the potatoes in a saucepan of lightly salted boiling water for 10 minutes, or until cooked through. Drain thoroughly and place in a mixing bowl.

3 Meanwhile, put the spinach in a saucepan with 2 tbsp of water, cover and cook over a low heat for 2 minutes, until wilted. Drain the spinach thoroughly, squeezing out excess moisture, and add to the potato.

4 Stir in the chopped tomato, chilli powder and lemon juice. Season to taste with salt and pepper.

5 Lightly brush 8 sheets of filo pastry with melted butter. Spread out 4 of the sheets and lay the other 4 on top of each. Cut them into rectangles about 20 x 10 cm/8 x 4 inches.

6 Spoon the potato and spinach mixture on to one end of each rectangle. Fold a corner of the pastry over the filling, fold the pointed end back over the pastry strip, then fold over the remaining pastry to form a triangle.

7 Place the triangles on the baking tray (cookie sheet) and bake in a preheated oven, 190°C/375°F/Gas Mark 5, for 20 minutes, or until golden brown.

8 To make the mayonnaise, mix the mayonnaise, lemon juice and lemon rind together in a small bowl. Serve the potato and spinach filo triangles warm or cold with the lemon mayonnaise and a crisp salad.

Spicy Potatoes & Onions

Masala aloo are potatoes cooked in spices and onions. Semi-dry when cooked, they make an excellent accompaniment to almost any curry.

NUTRITIONAL INFORMATION

Calories	.313	Sugars	.5g
Protein	.2g	Fat	.25g
Carbohydrate	.21g	Saturates	.3g

  10-15 MINS 10 MINS

SERVES 4

INGREDIENTS

6 tbsp vegetable oil

2 medium-sized onions,
   finely chopped

1 tsp finely chopped
   root ginger

1 tsp crushed garlic

1 tsp chilli powder

1½ tsp ground cumin

1½ tsp ground coriander

1 tsp salt

400 g/14 oz can new potatoes

1 tbsp lemon juice

BAGHAAR

3 tbsp oil

3 dried red chillies

½ tsp onion seeds

½ tsp mustard seeds

½ tsp fenugreek seeds

TO GARNISH

fresh coriander (cilantro) leaves

1 green chilli, finely chopped

1 Heat the oil in a large, heavy-based saucepan. Add the onions and fry, stirring, until golden brown. Reduce the heat, add the ginger, garlic, chilli powder, ground cumin, ground coriander and salt and stir-fry for about 1 minute. Remove the pan from the heat and set aside until required.

2 Drain the water from the potatoes. Add the potatoes to the onion and spice mixture and heat through. Sprinkle over the lemon juice and mix well.

3 To make the baghaar, heat the oil in a separate pan. Add the red chillies, onion seeds, mustard seeds and fenugreek seeds and fry until the seeds turn a shade darker. Remove the pan from the heat and pour the baghaar over the potatoes.

4 Garnish with coriander (cilantro) leaves and chillies, then serve.

Chilli Roast Potatoes

Small new potatoes are scrubbed and boiled in their skins, before being coated in a chilli mixture and roasted to perfection in the oven.

NUTRITIONAL INFORMATION

Calories 178	Sugars 2g
Protein 2g	Fat 11g
Carbohydrate ...18g	Saturates 1g

5-10 MINS   30 MINS

SERVES 4

INGREDIENTS

500 g/1 lb 2 oz small new potatoes,
  scrubbed

150 ml/¼ pint/⅔ cup vegetable oil

1 tsp chilli powder

½ tsp caraway seeds

1 tsp salt

1 tbsp chopped basil

1 Cook the potatoes in a saucepan of boiling water for 10 minutes, then drain thoroughly.

2 Pour a little of the oil into a shallow roasting tin (pan) to coat the base. Heat the oil in a preheated oven, 200°C/400°F/Gas Mark 6, for 10 minutes. Add the potatoes to the tin (pan) and brush them with the hot oil.

3 In a small bowl, mix together the chilli powder, caraway seeds and salt. Sprinkle the mixture over the potatoes, turning to coat them all over.

4 Add the remaining oil to the tin (pan) and roast in the oven for about 15 minutes, or until the potatoes are cooked through.

5 Using a slotted spoon, remove the potatoes from the the oil, draining them well and transfer them to a warmed serving dish. Sprinkle the chopped basil over the top and serve immediately.

VARIATION

Use any other spice of your choice, such as curry powder or paprika, for a variation in flavour.

Potatoes Dauphinois

This is a classic potato dish of layered potatoes, cream, garlic, onion and cheese. Serve with pies, bakes and casseroles.

NUTRITIONAL INFORMATION

Calories 580	Sugars 5g
Protein 10g	Fat 46g
Carbohydrate ...34g	Saturates 28g

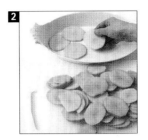

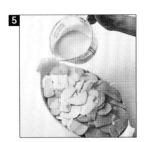

 25 MINS   1½ HOURS

SERVES 4

I N G R E D I E N T S

15 g/½ oz/1 tbsp butter

675 g/1½ lb waxy potatoes, sliced

2 garlic cloves, crushed

1 red onion, sliced

90 g/3 oz/¾ cup grated Gruyère (Swiss) cheese

300 ml/½ pint/1¼ cups double (heavy) cream

salt and pepper

1 Lightly grease a 1 litre/1¾ pint/ 4 cup shallow ovenproof dish with the butter.

2 Arrange a single layer of potato slices in the base of the prepared dish.

3 Top the potato slices with half the garlic, half the sliced red onion and one-third of the grated Gruyère (Swiss) cheese. Season to taste with a little salt and pepper.

4 Repeat the layers in exactly the same order, finishing with a layer of potatoes topped with grated cheese.

5 Pour the cream over the top of the potatoes and cook in a preheated oven, 180°C/350°F/Gas Mark 4, for 1½ hours, or until the potatoes are cooked through and the top is browned and crispy. Serve at once, straight from the dish.

COOK'S TIP

There are many versions of this classic potato dish, but the different recipes always contain double (heavy) cream, making it a rich and very filling side dish or accompaniment. This recipe must be cooked in a shallow dish to ensure there is plenty of crispy topping.

Souffléd Cheesy Potato Fries

These small potato chunks are mixed in a creamy cheese sauce and fried in oil until deliciously golden brown.

NUTRITIONAL INFORMATION

Calories 614   Sugars 2g
Protein . . . . .12g   Fat 46g
Carbohydrate . . .40g   Saturates 18g

 20 MINS   25 MINS

SERVES 4

INGREDIENTS

900 g/2 lb potatoes, cut
    into chunks

150 ml/¼ pint/⅔ cup double (heavy) cream

75 g/2¾ oz/¾ cup grated Gruyère
    (Swiss) cheese

pinch of cayenne pepper

2 egg whites

oil, for deep-frying

salt and pepper

chopped flat leaf parsley and grated
    cheese, to garnish

1 Cook the potatoes in a saucepan of boiling lightly salted water for about 10 minutes. Drain thoroughly and pat dry with absorbent kitchen paper (paper towels). Set aside until required.

2 Mix the double (heavy) cream and Gruyère (Swiss) cheese in a large bowl. Stir in the cayenne pepper and season with salt and pepper to taste.

3 Whisk the egg whites until stiff peaks form. Gently fold into the cheese mixture until fully incorporated.

4 Add the cooked potatoes, turning to coat thoroughly in the mixture.

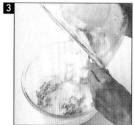

5 Heat the oil for deep-frying to 180°C/350°F or until a cube of bread browns in 30 seconds. Remove the potatoes from the cheese mixture with a slotted spoon and cook in the oil, in batches, if necessary, for 3–4 minutes, or until golden.

6 Transfer the potatoes to a warmed serving dish and garnish with parsley and grated cheese. Serve immediately.

VARIATION

Add other flavourings, such as grated nutmeg or curry powder, to the cream and cheese.

Saffron-Flavoured Potatoes

Saffron is made from the dried stigma of the crocus and is native to Greece. It is very expensive, but only a very small amount is needed.

NUTRITIONAL INFORMATION

Calories 197   Sugars 4g
Protein . . . . .4g   Fat 6g
Carbohydrate . . .30g   Saturates 1g

 25 MINS   40 MINS

SERVES 4

I N G R E D I E N T S

1 tsp saffron strands

6 tbsp boiling water

675 g/1½ lb waxy potatoes,
    unpeeled and cut into wedges

1 red onion, cut into 8 wedges

2 garlic cloves, crushed

1 tbsp white wine vinegar

2 tbsp olive oil

1 tbsp wholegrain mustard

5 tbsp vegetable stock

5 tbsp dry white wine

2 tsp chopped rosemary

salt and pepper

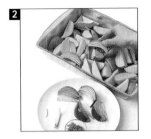

1 Place the saffron strands in a small bowl and pour over the boiling water. Set aside to soak for about 10 minutes.

2 Place the potatoes in a roasting tin (pan), together with the red onion wedges and crushed garlic.

3 Add the vinegar, oil, mustard, vegetable stock, white wine, rosemary and saffron water to the potatoes and onion in the tin (pan). Season to taste with salt and pepper.

4 Cover the roasting tin (pan) with kitchen foil and bake in a preheated oven, 200°C/400°F/Gas Mark 6, for 30 minutes.

5 Remove the foil and cook the potatoes for a further 10 minutes until crisp, browned and cooked through. Serve hot.

COOK'S TIP

Turmeric may be used instead of saffron to provide the yellow colour in this recipe. However, it is worth using saffron, if possible, for the lovely nutty flavour it gives a dish.

Candied Sweet Potatoes

A taste of the Caribbean is introduced in this recipe, where sweet potatoes are cooked with sugar and lime with a dash of brandy.

NUTRITIONAL INFORMATION

Calories . . . . . . .348 Sugars 21g
Protein . . . . .3g Fat 9g
Carbohydrate . . .67g Saturates 6g

 15 MINS   🕐 25 MINS

SERVES 4

I N G R E D I E N T S

675 g/1½ lb sweet potatoes, sliced

40 g/1½ oz/3 tbsp butter

1 tbsp lime juice

75 g/2¾ oz/½ cup soft dark brown sugar

1 tbsp brandy

grated rind of 1 lime

lime wedges, to garnish

1 Cook the sweet potatoes in a saucepan of boiling water for about 5 minutes. Test the potatoes have softened by pricking with a fork. Remove the sweet potatoes with a perforated spoon and drain thoroughly.

2 Melt the butter in a large frying pan (skillet). Add the lime juice and brown sugar and heat gently, stirring, to dissolve the sugar.

3 Stir the sweet potatoes and the brandy into the sugar and lime juice mixture. Cook over a low heat for about 10 minutes or until the potato slices are cooked through.

4 Sprinkle the lime rind over the top of the sweet potatoes and mix well.

5 Transfer the candied sweet potatoes to a serving plate. Garnish with lime wedges and serve at once.

COOK'S TIP

Sweet potatoes have a pinkish skin and either white, yellow or orange flesh. It doesn't matter which type is used for this dish.

Curried Roast Potatoes

This is the kind of Indian-inspired dish that would fit easily into any Western menu, or how about serving with a curry in place of rice?

NUTRITIONAL INFORMATION

Calories ....297 Sugars 2g
Protein ....3g Fat 19g
Carbohydrate ...30g Saturates 12g

  5 MINS   30–35 MINS

SERVES 4

I N G R E D I E N T S

2 tsp cumin seeds

2 tsp coriander seeds

90 g/3 oz/6 tbsp butter

1 tsp ground turmeric

1 tsp black mustard seeds

2 garlic cloves, crushed

2 dried red chillies

750 g/1 lb 10 oz baby new potatoes

1 Grind the cumin and coriander seeds together in a mortar with a pestle or spice grinder. Grinding them fresh like this captures all of the flavour before it has a chance to dry out.

2 Melt the butter gently in a roasting tin (pan) and add the turmeric, mustard seeds, garlic and chillies and the ground cumin and coriander seeds. Stir well to combine evenly. Place in a preheated oven at 200°C/400°F/Gas Mark 6 for 5 minutes.

3 Remove the tin (pan) from the oven – the spices should be very fragrant at this stage – and add the potatoes. Stir well so that the butter and spice mix coats the potatoes completely.

4 Return to the oven and bake for 20–25 minutes. Stir occasionally to ensure that the potatoes are coated evenly. Test the potatoes with a skewer – if they drop off the end of the skewer when lifted, they are done. Transfer to a serving dish and serve immediately.

COOK'S TIP

Baby new potatoes are now available all year round from supermarkets. However, they are not essential for this recipe. Red or white old potatoes can be substituted, cut into 2.5 cm/1 inch cubes. You can also try substituting parsnips, carrots or turnips, cut into 2.5 cm/1 inch cubes.

Bombay Potatoes

Although virtually unknown in India, this dish is a very popular item on Indian restaurant menus in other parts of the world.

NUTRITIONAL INFORMATION

Calories	307	Sugars	.........9g
Protein	.........9g	Fat	..........9g
Carbohydrate	...51g	Saturates	.......5g

5 MINS   1 HR 10 MINS

SERVES 4

INGREDIENTS

1 kg/2 lb 4 oz waxy potatoes

2 tbsp vegetable ghee

1 tsp panch poran spice mix

3 tsp ground turmeric

2 tbsp tomato purée (paste)

300 ml/½ pint/1¼ cups natural (unsweetened) yogurt

salt

chopped coriander (cilantro), to garnish

1 Put the whole potatoes into a large saucepan of salted cold water, bring to the boil, then simmer until the potatoes are just cooked, but not tender; the time depends on the size of the potato, but an average-sized one should take about 15 minutes.

COOK'S TIP

Panch poran spice mix can be bought from Asian or Indian grocery stores, or make your own from equal quantities of cumin seeds, fennel seeds, mustard seeds, nigella seeds and fenugreek seeds.

2 Heat the ghee in a saucepan over a medium heat and add the panch poran, turmeric, tomato purée (paste), yogurt and salt. Bring to the boil, and simmer, uncovered, for 5 minutes.

3 Drain the potatoes and cut each one into 4 pieces. Add the potatoes to the pan, cover and cook briefly. Transfer to an ovenproof casserole, cover and cook in a preheated oven, 180°C/350°F/Gas Mark 4, for about 40 minutes, or until the potatoes are tender and the sauce has thickened a little.

4 Sprinkle with chopped coriander (cilantro) and serve immediately.

Caramelized New Potatoes

This simple recipe is best served with a plainly cooked main course, as it is fairly sweet and has delicious juices.

NUTRITIONAL INFORMATION

Calories 289	Sugars 18g
Protein 3g	Fat 13g
Carbohydrate ...43g	Saturates 8g

 5 MINS   20 MINS

SERVES 4

INGREDIENTS

675 g/1½ lb new potatoes, scrubbed

4 tbsp dark brown sugar

60 g/2 oz/¼ cup butter

1 tbsp orange juice

1 tbsp chopped fresh parsley or
   coriander (cilantro)

salt and pepper

orange rind curls, to garnish

1 Cook the new potatoes in a saucepan of boiling water for 10 minutes, or until almost tender. Drain thoroughly.

2 Melt the sugar in a large, heavy-based frying pan (skillet) over a low heat, stirring constantly.

3 Add the butter and orange juice to the pan, stirring the mixture constantly as the butter melts.

4 Add the potatoes to the orange and butter mixture and continue to cook, turning the potatoes frequently until they are completely coated in the caramel.

5 Sprinkle the chopped parsley or coriander (cilantro) over the potatoes and season according to taste with salt and pepper.

6 Transfer the caramelized new potatoes to a serving dish and garnish with the orange rind. Serve immediately.

VARIATION

Lemon or lime juices may be used instead of the orange juice. In addition, garnish the finished dish with pared lemon or lime rind, if preferred.

Fried Spiced Potatoes

Deliciously good and a super accompaniment to almost any main course dish, although rather high in calories!

NUTRITIONAL INFORMATION

Calories 430	Sugars 7g
Protein 4g	Fat 35g
Carbohydrate . . .26g	Saturates 11g

 15 MINS   30 MINS

SERVES 6

I N G R E D I E N T S

2 onions, quartered

5 cm/2 inch piece of root ginger,
   finely chopped

2 garlic cloves

2–3 tbsp mild or medium curry paste

4 tbsp water

750 g/1 lb 10 oz new potatoes

vegetable oil, for deep frying

3 tbsp vegetable ghee or oil

150 ml/¼ pint/⅔ cup strained Greek yogurt

150 ml/¼ pint/⅔ cup double (heavy) cream

3 tbsp chopped mint

salt and pepper

½ bunch spring onions (scallions), chopped,
   to garnish

COOK'S TIP

When buying new potatoes, look for the freshest you can find. The skin should be beginning to rub off. Cook them as soon after purchase as possible, but if you have to store them, keep them in a cool, dark well-ventilated place.

1 Place the onions, ginger, garlic, curry paste and water in a blender or food processor and process until smooth, scraping down the sides of the machine and processing again, if necessary.

2 Cut the potatoes into quarters – the pieces need to be about 2.5 cm/1 inch in size – and pat dry with absorbent kitchen paper (paper towels). Heat the oil in a deep fryer to 180°C/350°F/Gas 4 or until a cube of bread browns in 30 seconds and fry the potatoes, in batches, for about 5 minutes or until golden brown, turning frequently. Remove from the pan and drain on kitchen paper (paper towels).

3 Heat the ghee or oil in a large frying pan (skillet), add the curry and onion mixture and fry gently, stirring constantly, for 2 minutes. Add the yogurt, cream and 2 tablespoons of mint and mix well.

4 Add the fried potatoes and stir until coated in the sauce. Cook, stirring frequently, for a further 5–7 minutes, or until heated through and sauce has thickened. Season with salt and pepper to taste and sprinkle with the remaining mint and sliced spring onions (scallions). Serve immediately.

Herby Potatoes & Onion

Fried potatoes are a classic favourite; here they are given extra flavour by frying them in butter with onion, garlic and herbs.

NUTRITIONAL INFORMATION

Calories 413	Sugars 4g
Protein 5g	Fat 26g
Carbohydrate . . .42g	Saturates 17g

 10 MINS

50 MINS

SERVES 4

INGREDIENTS

900 g/2 lb waxy potatoes, cut into cubes

125 g/4½ oz/½ cup butter

1 red onion, cut into 8

2 garlic cloves, crushed

1 tsp lemon juice

2 tbsp chopped thyme

salt and pepper

1 Cook the cubed potatoes in a saucepan of boiling water for 10 minutes. Drain thoroughly.

2 Melt the butter in a large, heavy-based frying pan (skillet) and add the red onion wedges, garlic and lemon juice. Cook, stirring constantly for 2–3 minutes.

3 Add the potatoes to the pan and mix well to coat in the butter mixture.

4 Reduce the heat, cover and cook for 25–30 minutes, or until the potatoes are golden brown and tender.

5 Sprinkle the chopped thyme over the top of the potatoes and season.

6 Transfer to a warm serving dish and serve immediately.

COOK'S TIP

Keep checking the potatoes and stirring throughout the cooking time to ensure that they do not burn or stick to the base of the frying pan (skillet).

Spicy Indian Potatoes

The potato is widely used in Indian cooking and there are many variations of spicy potatoes.

NUTRITIONAL INFORMATION

Calories 173   Sugars 6g
Protein . . . . .7g   Fat 9g
Carbohydrate . . .18g   Saturates 1g

15 MINS   40 MINS

SERVES 6

I N G R E D I E N T S

½ tsp coriander seeds

1 tsp cumin seeds

4 tbsp vegetable oil

2 cardamom pods

1 cm/½ inch piece of root ginger, grated

1 red chilli, chopped

1 onion, chopped

2 garlic cloves, crushed

500 g/1 lb 2 oz new potatoes, quartered

150 ml/¼ pint/⅔ cup vegetable stock

675 g/1½ lb spinach, chopped

4 tbsp natural (unsweetened) yogurt

salt

1 Grind the coriander and cumin seeds using a pestle and mortar.

2 Heat the oil in a frying pan (skillet). Add the ground coriander and cumin seeds to the pan, together with the cardamom pods and ginger and cook for about 2 minutes.

3 Add the chopped chilli, onion and garlic to the pan. Cook, stirring frequently, for a further 2 minutes.

4 Add the potatoes to the pan, together with the vegetable stock. Cook gently,

stirring occasionally, for 30 minutes, or until the potatoes are cooked through.

5 Add the spinach to the pan and cook for a further 5 minutes.

6 Remove the pan from the heat and stir in the yogurt. Season with salt and pepper to taste. Transfer the potatoes and spinach to a warmed serving dish and serve immediately.

VARIATION

Use frozen spinach instead of fresh spinach, if you prefer. Thaw the frozen spinach and drain it thoroughly before adding it to the dish, otherwise it will turn soggy.

Potatoes, Olives & Anchovies

This side dish makes a delicious accompaniment for grilled (broiled) fish or for lamb chops. The fennel adds a subtle aniseed flavour.

NUTRITIONAL INFORMATION

Calories 202	Sugars 2g	
Protein 7g	Fat 12g	
Carbohydrate ...19g	Saturates 1g	

 10 MINS   30 MINS

SERVES 4

I N G R E D I E N T S

450 g/1 lb baby new potatoes, scrubbed

2 tbsp olive oil

2 fennel bulbs, trimmed and sliced

2 sprigs rosemary, stalks removed

75 g/2¾ oz mixed olives

8 canned anchovy fillets, drained and
   chopped

1 Bring a large saucepan of water to the boil and cook the potatoes for 8–10 minutes or until tender. Remove the potatoes from the saucepan using a perforated spoon and set aside to cool slightly.

2 Once the potatoes are just cool enough to handle, cut them into wedges, using a sharp knife.

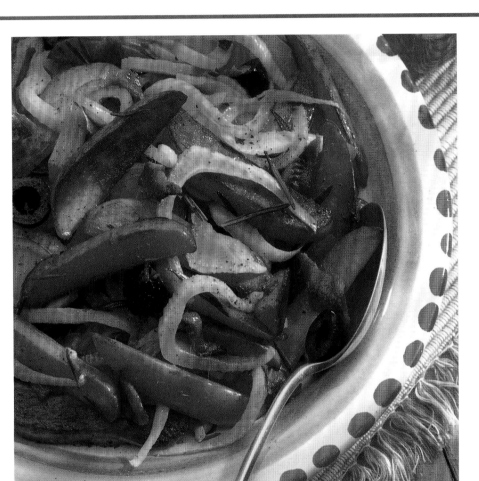

3 Pit the mixed olives and cut them in half, using a sharp knife.

4 Using a sharp knife, chop the anchovy fillets into smaller strips.

5 Heat the oil in a large frying pan (skillet). Add the potato wedges, sliced fennel and rosemary. Cook for 7–8 minutes or until the potatoes are golden.

6 Stir in the olives and anchovies and cook for 1 minute or until completely warmed through.

7 Transfer to serving plates and serve immediately.

COOK'S TIP

Fresh rosemary is a particular favourite with Italians, but you can experiment with your favourite herbs in this recipe, if you prefer.

Pesto Potatoes

Pesto sauce is more commonly used as a pasta sauce but is delicious served over potatoes as well.

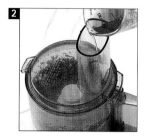

NUTRITIONAL INFORMATION

Calories	531	Sugars	. . . . .3g
Protein	. . . . .13g	Fat	. . . . .38g
Carbohydrate	. . .36g	Saturates	. . . . .8g

 15 MINS 15 MINS

SERVES 4

I N G R E D I E N T S

900 g/2 lb small new potatoes

75 g/2¾ oz fresh basil

2 tbsp pine kernels (nuts)

3 garlic cloves, crushed

100 ml/3½ fl oz/½ cup olive oil

75 g/2¾ oz/¾ cup freshly grated Parmesan
    cheese and Pecorino cheese, mixed

salt and pepper

fresh basil sprigs, to garnish

1 Cook the potatoes in a saucepan of boiling salted water for 15 minutes or until tender. Drain well, transfer to a warm serving dish and keep warm until required.

2 Meanwhile, put the basil, pine kernels (nuts), garlic and a little salt and pepper to taste in a food processor. Blend for 30 seconds, adding the oil gradually, until smooth.

3 Remove the mixture from the food processor and place in a mixing bowl. Stir in the grated Parmesan and Pecorino cheeses.

4 Spoon the pesto sauce over the potatoes and mix well. Garnish with fresh basil sprigs and serve immediately.

Parmesan Potatoes

This is a very simple way to jazz up roast potatoes. Serve them in the same way as roast potatoes with roasted meats or fish.

NUTRITIONAL INFORMATION

Calories 307	Sugars 2g
Protein 11g	Fat 14g
Carbohydrate . . .37g	Saturates 6g

15 MINS   1 HR 5 MINS

SERVES 4

INGREDIENTS

6 potatoes

50 g/1¾ oz Parmesan cheese, grated

pinch of grated nutmeg

1 tbsp chopped fresh parsley

4 smoked bacon slices, cut into strips

oil, for roasting

salt

1 Cut the potatoes in half lengthways and cook them in a saucepan of boiling salted water for 10 minutes. Drain thoroughly.

2 Mix the grated Parmesan cheese, nutmeg and parsley together in a shallow bowl.

3 Roll the potato pieces in the cheese mixture to coat them completely. Shake off any excess.

VARIATION

If you prefer, use slices of salami or Parma ham (prosciutto) instead of the bacon, adding it to the dish 5 minutes before the end of the cooking time.

4 Pour a little oil into a roasting tin (pan) and heat it in a preheated oven, 200°C/400°F/Gas Mark 6, for 10 minutes. Remove from the oven and place the potatoes into the tin (pan). Return the tin (pan) to the oven and cook for 30 minutes, turning once.

5 Remove from the oven and sprinkle the bacon on top of the potatoes. Return to the oven for 15 minutes or until the potatoes and bacon are cooked. Drain off any excess fat and serve.

Lemony & Herby Potatoes

Choose from these two divine recipes for new potatoes. To check if new potatoes are fresh, rub the skin; the skin will come off easily if fresh.

NUTRITIONAL INFORMATION

Calories ......226 Sugars 2g
Protein ....5g Fat 5g
Carbohydrate ...42g Saturates 3g

🥔 20 MINS   🕐 35 MINS

SERVES 4

INGREDIENTS

LEMONY NEW POTATOES

1 kg/2 lb 4 oz new potatoes

25 g/1 oz/2 tbsp butter

1 tbsp finely grated lemon rind

2 tbsp lemon juice

1 tbsp chopped fresh dill or chives

salt and pepper

extra chopped fresh dill or chives, to garnish

HERBY NEW POTATOES

1 kg/2 lb 4 oz new potatoes

3 tbsp light olive oil

1 tbsp white wine vinegar

pinch of dry mustard

pinch of caster (superfine) sugar

salt and pepper

2 tbsp chopped mixed fresh herbs, such as parsley, chives, marjoram, basil and rosemary

extra chopped fresh mixed herbs, to garnish

1 For the lemony potatoes, either scrub the potatoes well or remove the skins by scraping them off with a sharp knife. Cook the potatoes in plenty of lightly salted boiling water for about 15 minutes, until just tender.

2 While the potatoes are cooking, melt the butter over a low heat. Add the lemon rind, juice and herbs. Season with salt and pepper.

3 Drain the cooked potatoes and transfer to a serving bowl.

4 Pour over the lemony butter mixture and stir gently to mix. Garnish with extra herbs and serve hot or warm.

5 For the herby potatoes, prepare and cook the potatoes as described in step 1. Whisk the oil, vinegar, mustard, caster (superfine) sugar and seasoning together in a small bowl. Add the chopped herbs and mix well.

6 Drain the potatoes and pour over the oil and vinegar mixture, stirring to coat evenly. Garnish with extra fresh herbs and serve warm or cold.

Trio of Potato Purées

These small moulds (molds) filled with layers of flavoured potato look very impressive. They are ideal with fish or roast meats.

NUTRITIONAL INFORMATION

Calories 170   Sugars 5g
Protein . . . . .7g   Fat 6g
Carbohydrate . . .24g   Saturates 3g

15 MINS   1¼ HOURS

SERVES 4

I N G R E D I E N T S

300 g/10½ oz floury (mealy) potatoes, chopped

125 g/4½ oz swede, chopped

1 carrot, chopped

450 g/1 lb spinach

1 tbsp skimmed milk

15 g/½ oz/1 tbsp butter

25 g/1 oz/¼ cup plain (all purpose) flour

1 egg

½ tsp ground cinnamon

1 tbsp orange juice

¼ tsp grated nutmeg

salt and pepper

carrot matchsticks, to garnish

1 Lightly grease four 150 ml/¼ pint/ ⅔ cup ramekins.

2 Cook the potatoes in a saucepan of boiling water for 10 minutes. In separate pans cook the swede and carrot in boiling water for 10 minutes. Blanch the spinach in boiling water for 5 minutes. Drain the vegetables. Add the milk and butter to the potatoes and mash until smooth. Stir in the flour and egg.

3 Divide the potato mixture into 3 bowls. Spoon the swede into one bowl and mix well. Spoon the carrot into the second bowl and mix well. Spoon the spinach into the third bowl and mix well.

4 Add the cinnamon to the swede and potato mixture and season to taste. Stir the orange juice into the carrot and potato mixture. Stir the nutmeg into the spinach and potato mixture.

5 Spoon a layer of the swede and potato mixture into each of the ramekins and smooth over the top. Cover each with a layer of spinach and potato mixture, then top with the carrot and potato mixture. Cover the ramekins with foil and place in a roasting tin (pan). Half fill the tin (pan) with boiling water and cook in a preheated oven, 180°C/350°F/Gas Mark 4, for 40 minutes or until set.

6 Turn out on to serving plates, garnish with the carrot matchsticks and serve immediately.

Potato & Radish Salad

The radishes and the herb and mustard dressing give this colourful salad a mild mustard flavour which complements the potatoes perfectly.

NUTRITIONAL INFORMATION

Calories	140	Sugars	.........3g
Protein	.........3g	Fat	...........6g
Carbohydrate	...20g	Saturates	.......1g

 50 MINS   20 MINS

SERVES 4

INGREDIENTS

500 g/1 lb 2 oz new potatoes, scrubbed
  and halved

½ cucumber, thinly sliced

2 tsp salt

1 bunch radishes, thinly sliced

DRESSING

1 tbsp Dijon mustard

2 tbsp olive oil

1 tbsp white wine vinegar

2 tbsp mixed chopped herbs

1 Cook the potatoes in a saucepan of boiling water for 10–15 minutes, or until tender. Drain and set aside to cool.

2 Meanwhile, spread out the cucumber slices on a plate and sprinkle with the salt. Leave to stand for 30 minutes, then rinse under cold running water and pat dry with kitchen paper (paper towels).

3 Arrange the cucumber and radish slices on a serving plate in a decorative pattern and pile the cooked potatoes in the centre of the slices.

4 In a small bowl, mix all the dressing ingredients together, whisking until thoroughly combined. Pour the dressing over the salad, tossing well to coat all of the ingredients. Chill in the refrigerator before serving.

COOK'S TIP

The cucumber adds not only colour, but also a real freshness to the salad. It is salted and left to stand to remove the excess water, which would make the salad soggy. Wash the cucumber well to remove all of the salt, before adding to the salad.

Three-Way Potato Salad

Small new potatoes, served warm in a delicious dressing. The nutritional information is for the potato salad with the curry dressing only.

NUTRITIONAL INFORMATION

Calories 310	Sugars 12g
Protein 6g	Fat 19g
Carbohydrate . . .31g	Saturates 4g

 15-20 MINS   20 MINS

SERVES 4

I N G R E D I E N T S

500 g/1 lb 2 oz new potatoes (for each
  dressing)

herbs, to garnish

LIGHT CURRY DRESSING

1 tbsp vegetable oil

1 tbsp medium curry paste

1 small onion, chopped

1 tbsp mango chutney, chopped

6 tbsp natural (unsweetened) yogurt

3 tbsp single (light) cream

2 tbsp mayonnaise

salt and pepper

1 tbsp single (light) cream, to garnish

VINAIGRETTE DRESSING

6 tbsp hazelnut oil

3 tbsp cider vinegar

1 tsp wholegrain mustard

1 tsp caster (superfine) sugar

few basil leaves, torn

PARSLEY CREAM

150 ml/¼ pint/⅔ cup soured cream

3 tbsp light mayonnaise

4 spring onions (scallions), finely chopped

1 tbsp chopped fresh parsley

1 To make the Light Curry Dressing, heat the vegetable oil in a saucepan, add the curry paste and onion and fry, stirring frequently, until the onion is soft. Remove from the heat and set aside to cool slightly.

2 Mix together the mango chutney, yogurt, cream and mayonnaise. Add the curry mixture and blend together. Season with salt and pepper.

3 To make the Vinaigrette Dressing, whisk the oil, vinegar, mustard, sugar and basil together in a small jug or bowl. Season with salt and pepper.

4 To make the Parsley Cream, combine the mayonnaise, soured cream, spring onions (scallions) and parsley, mixing well. Season with salt and pepper.

5 Cook the potatoes in lightly salted boiling water until just tender. Drain well and set aside to cool for 5 minutes, then add the chosen dressing, tossing to coat. Serve, garnished with fresh herbs, spooning a little single (light) cream on to the potatoes if you have used the curry dressing.

Garden Salad

This chunky salad includes tiny new potatoes tossed in a minty dressing, and has a mustard dip for dunking.

NUTRITIONAL INFORMATION

Calories . . . . . . .227 Sugars 6g
Protein . . . . .4g Fat 17g
Carbohydrate . . .16g Saturates 4g

15–20 MINS   20 MINS

SERVES 8

I N G R E D I E N T S

500 g/1 lb 2 oz tiny new or salad potatoes
225 g/8 oz broccoli florets
125 g/4½ oz sugar snap peas
2 large carrots
4 celery sticks
1 yellow or orange (bell) pepper, seeded
1 bunch spring onions (scallions)
1 head chicory (endive)

D R E S S I N G
3 tbsp olive oil
1 tbsp white wine vinegar
1 tsp Dijon mustard
2 tbsp chopped mint

M U S T A R D   D I P
6 tbsp soured cream
3 tbsp thick mayonnaise
2 tsp balsamic vinegar
1½ tsp coarse-grain mustard
½ tsp creamed horseradish
pinch of brown sugar
salt and pepper

1 Cook the potatoes in boiling salted water for about 10 minutes, until just tender. While they cook, combine the dressing ingredients.

2 Drain the potatoes thoroughly, add to the dressing while hot, toss well and set aside until cold, giving them an occasional stir.

3 To make the dip, combine the soured cream, mayonnaise, vinegar, mustard, horseradish and sugar and season to taste with salt and pepper. Transfer to a small serving bowl, cover and refrigerate until ready to serve.

4 Cut the broccoli into bite-sized florets and blanch for 2 minutes in boiling water. Drain and toss immediately in cold water; when cold, drain thoroughly.

5 Blanch the sugar snap peas in boiling water for 1 minute. Drain, rinse in cold water and drain again.

6 Cut the carrots and celery into matchsticks about 6 x 1 cm/2½ x ½ inches. Slice the (bell) pepper or cut it into small cubes. Cut off some of the green parts of the spring onions (scallions) and separate the chicory (endive) leaves.

7 Arrange the vegetables attractively in a fairly shallow bowl with the potatoes piled up in the centre. Serve accompanied with the mustard dip.

Potatoes in Italian Dressing

The warm potatoes quickly absorb the wonderful flavours of olives, tomatoes and olive oil. This salad is good warm and cold.

NUTRITIONAL INFORMATION

Calories	239	Sugars	.........2g
Protein	.........4g	Fat	..........10g
Carbohydrate	...36g	Saturates	.......1g

 15 MINS   🕐 15 MINS

SERVES 4

I N G R E D I E N T S

750 g/1 lb 10 oz waxy potatoes

1 shallot

2 tomatoes

1 tbsp chopped fresh basil

salt

I T A L I A N   D R E S S I N G

1 tomato, skinned and chopped finely

4 black olives, pitted and chopped finely

4 tbsp olive oil

1 tbsp wine vinegar

1 garlic clove, crushed

salt and pepper

1 Cook the potatoes in a saucepan of boiling salted water for 15 minutes or until they are tender.

2 Drain the potatoes well, chop roughly and put into a bowl.

3 Chop the shallot. Cut the tomatoes into wedges and add the shallot and tomatoes to the potatoes.

4 To make the dressing, put all the ingredients into a screw-top jar and mix together thoroughly.

5 Pour the dressing over the potato mixture and toss thoroughly.

6 Transfer the salad to a serving dish and sprinkle with the basil.

COOK'S TIP

This recipe works well with floury (mealy) potatoes. It doesn't look so attractive, as the potatoes break up when they are cooked, but they absorb the dressing wonderfully. Be sure to use an extra virgin olive oil for the dressing to give a really fruity flavour to the potatoes.

Potato & Sausage Salad

Sliced Italian sausage blends well with the other Mediterranean flavours of sun-dried tomato and basil in this salad.

NUTRITIONAL INFORMATION

Calories 450   Sugars 6g
Protein . . . . .13g   Fat 28g
Carbohydrate . . .38g   Saturates 1g

25 MINS   25 MINS

SERVES 4

INGREDIENTS

450 g/1 lb waxy potatoes

1 raddichio or lollo rosso lettuce

1 green (bell) pepper, sliced

175 g/6 oz Italian sausage, sliced

1 red onion, halved and sliced

125 g/4½ oz sun-dried tomatoes, sliced

2 tbsp shredded fresh basil

DRESSING

1 tbsp balsamic vinegar

1 tsp tomato purée (paste)

2 tbsp olive oil

salt and pepper

COOK'S TIP

Any sliced Italian sausage or salami can be used in this salad. Italy is home of the salami and there are numerous varieties to choose from – those from the south tend to be more highly spiced than those from the north of the country.

1 Cook the potatoes in a saucepan of boiling water for 20 minutes or until cooked through. Drain and leave to cool.

2 Line a large serving platter with the radicchio or lollo rosso lettuce leaves.

3 Slice the cooled potatoes and arrange them in layers on the lettuce-lined serving platter together with the sliced green (bell) pepper, sliced Italian sausage, red onion, sun-dried tomatoes and shredded fresh basil.

4 In a small bowl, whisk the balsamic vinegar, tomato purée (paste) and olive oil together and season to taste with salt and pepper. Pour the dressing over the potato salad and serve immediately.

Italian Potato Salad

Potato salad is always a favourite, but it is even more delicious with the addition of sun-dried tomatoes and fresh parsley.

NUTRITIONAL INFORMATION

Calories 425	Sugars 6g	
Protein 6g	Fat 27g	
Carbohydrate . . .43g	Saturates 5g	

 40 MINS   15 MINS

SERVES 4

INGREDIENTS

450 g/1 lb baby potatoes, unpeeled, or
 larger potatoes, halved

4 tbsp natural yogurt

4 tbsp mayonnaise

8 sun-dried tomatoes

2 tbsp flat leaf parsley, chopped

salt and pepper

1 Rinse and clean the potatoes and place them in a large pan of water. Bring to the boil and cook for 8–12 minutes or until just tender. (The cooking time will vary according to the size of the potatoes.)

2 Using a sharp knife, cut the sun-dried tomatoes into thin slices.

3 To make the dressing, mix together the yogurt and mayonnaise in a bowl and season to taste with a little salt and pepper. Stir in the sun-dried tomato slices and the chopped flat leaf parsley.

4 Remove the potatoes with a perforated spoon, drain them thoroughly and then set them aside to cool. If you are using larger potatoes, cut them into 5 cm/2 inch chunks.

5 Pour the dressing over the potatoes and toss to mix.

6 Leave the potato salad to chill in the refrigerator for about 20 minutes, then serve as a starter or as an accompaniment.

COOK'S TIP

It is easier to cut the larger potatoes once they are cooked. Although smaller pieces of potato will cook more quickly, they tend to disintegrate and become mushy.

Potato & Cauliflower Curry

Potatoes and cauliflower go very well together. Served with a dhal and rice or bread, this dish makes a perfect vegetarian meal.

NUTRITIONAL INFORMATION

Calories ....426 Sugars 6g
Protein ....4g Fat 35g
Carbohydrate ...26g Saturates 4g

 10 MINS   25 MINS

SERVES 4

I N G R E D I E N T S

150 ml/¼ pint/⅔ cup vegetable oil

½ tsp white cumin seeds

4 dried red chillies

2 medium onions, sliced

1 tsp finely chopped root ginger

1 tsp crushed garlic

1 tsp chilli powder

1 tsp salt

pinch of turmeric

3 medium potatoes, chopped

½ cauliflower, cut into small florets

2 green chillies (optional)

coriander (cilantro) leaves

150 ml/¼ pint/⅔ cup water

 1 Heat the oil in a large heavy-based saucepan. Add the white cumin seeds and dried red chillies to the pan, stirring to mix.

2 Add the onions to the pan and fry over a medium heat, stirring occasionally, for about 5–8 minutes, until golden brown.

3 Mix the ginger, garlic, chilli powder, salt and turmeric together. Add the spice mixture to the onions and stir-fry for about 2 minutes.

4 Add the potatoes and cauliflower to the pan and stir to coat thoroughly with the spice mixture. Reduce the heat and add the green chillies (if using), coriander (cilantro) leaves and water to the pan. Cover and simmer for about 10-15 minutes, until the vegetables are cooked through and tender.

5 Transfer the potato and cauliflower curry to warmed serving plates and serve immediately.

COOK'S TIP

Ground ginger is no substitute for the fresh root. It is less aromatic and flavoursome and cannot be used in fried or sautéed dishes, as it burns easily at the high temperatures required.

Bubble & Squeak

Bubble and squeak is best known as fried mashed potato and leftover greens served as an accompaniment.

NUTRITIONAL INFORMATION

Calories 301   Sugars 5g
Protein . . . . .11g   Fat 18g
Carbohydrate . . .24g   Saturates 2g

15 MINS   40 MINS

SERVES 4

I N G R E D I E N T S

450 g/1 lb floury (mealy) potatoes, diced

225 g/8 oz Savoy cabbage, shredded

5 tbsp vegetable oil

2 leeks, chopped

1 garlic clove, crushed

225 g/8 oz smoked tofu (bean curd), cubed

salt and pepper

shredded cooked leek, to garnish

1 Cook the diced potatoes in a saucepan of lightly salted boiling water for 10 minutes, until tender. Drain and mash the potatoes.

2 Meanwhile, in a separate saucepan, blanch the cabbage in boiling water for 5 minutes. Drain well and add to the potato.

COOK'S TIP

This vegetarian version is a perfect main meal, as the smoked tofu (bean curd) cubes added to the basic bubble and squeak mixture make it very substantial and nourishing.

3 Heat the oil in a heavy-based frying pan (skillet). Add the leeks and garlic and fry gently for 2-3 minutes. Stir into the potato and cabbage mixture.

4 Add the smoked tofu (bean curd) and season well with salt and pepper. Cook over a moderate heat for 10 minutes.

5 Carefully turn the whole mixture over and continue to cook over a moderate heat for a further 5-7 minutes, until crispy underneath. Serve immediately, garnished with shredded leek.

Green Bean & Potato Curry

You can use fresh or canned green beans for this semi-dry vegetable curry. Serve an oil-dressed dhal for contrasting flavours and colours.

NUTRITIONAL INFORMATION

Calories . . . . . . .690 Sugars 4g
Protein . . . . .3g Fat 69g
Carbohydrate . . .16g Saturates 7g

15 MINS   30 MINS

SERVES 4

I N G R E D I E N T S

300 ml/½ pint/1¼ cups oil

1 tsp white cumin seeds

1 tsp mustard and onion seeds

4 dried red chillies

3 fresh tomatoes, sliced

1 tsp salt

1 tsp finely chopped root ginger

1 tsp crushed garlic

1 tsp chilli powder

200 g/7 oz green cut beans

2 medium potatoes, diced

300 ml/½ pint/1¼ cups water

coriander (cilantro) leaves, chopped

2 green chillies, finely chopped

boiled rice, to serve

1 Heat the oil in a large, heavy-based saucepan. Lower the heat and add the white cumin seeds, mustard and onion seeds and dried red chillies to the saucepan, stirring well.

2 Add the tomatoes to the pan and stir-fry the mixture for 3–5 minutes.

3 Mix together the salt, ginger, garlic and chilli powder and spoon into the pan. Blend the mixture together.

4 Add the green beans and potatoes to the pan and stir-fry for about 5 minutes.

5 Add the water to the pan, reduce the heat to low and simmer for 10–15 minutes, stirring occasionally.

6 Garnish the green bean and potato curry with chopped coriander (cilantro) leaves and green chillies and serve hot with boiled rice.

COOK'S TIP

Mustard seeds are often fried in oil or ghee to bring out their flavour before being combined with other ingredients.

Four-Cheese & Potato Layer

This is a quick dish to prepare and it can be left to cook in the oven without requiring any further attention.

NUTRITIONAL INFORMATION

Calories 766	Sugars 14g
Protein 44g	Fat 40g
Carbohydrate . . .60g	Saturates 23g

 25 MINS 45 MINS

SERVES 4

INGREDIENTS

900 g/2 lb unpeeled waxy potatoes,
   cut into wedges

25 g/1 oz/2 tbsp butter

1 red onion, halved and sliced

2 garlic cloves, crushed

25 g/1 oz/¼ cup plain (all-purpose) flour

600 ml/1 pint/2½ cups milk

400 g/14 oz can artichoke hearts in brine,
   drained and halved

150 g/5½ oz frozen mixed
   vegetables, thawed

125 g/4½ oz/1 cup grated Gruyère
   (Swiss) cheese

125 g/4½ oz/1 cup grated mature
   (sharp) cheese

50 g/1¾ oz/½ cup crumbled Gorgonzola

25 g/1 oz/⅓ cup grated Parmesan cheese

225 g/8 oz tofu (bean curd), sliced

2 tbsp chopped thyme

salt and pepper

thyme sprigs, to garnish

1 Cook the potato wedges in a saucepan of boiling water for 10 minutes. Drain thoroughly.

2 Meanwhile, melt the butter in a saucepan. Add the sliced onion and garlic and fry over a low heat, stirring frequently, for 2-3 minutes.

3 Stir the flour into the pan and cook for 1 minute. Gradually add the milk and bring to the boil, stirring constantly.

4 Reduce the heat and add the artichoke hearts, mixed vegetables, half of each of the 4 cheeses and the tofu (bean curd) to the pan, mixing well. Stir in the chopped thyme and season with salt and pepper to taste.

5 Arrange a layer of parboiled potato wedges in the base of a shallow ovenproof dish. Spoon the vegetable mixture over the top and cover with the remaining potato wedges. Sprinkle the rest of the 4 cheeses over the top.

6 Cook in a preheated oven, 200°C/400°F/Gas Mark 6, for 30 minutes or until the potatoes are cooked and the top is golden brown. Serve the bake garnished with fresh thyme sprigs.

Cheese Potato Cakes

Make these tasty potato cakes for a quick and simple supper dish. Serve them with scrambled eggs if you're very hungry.

NUTRITIONAL INFORMATION

Calories 766   Sugars 7g
Protein . . . . .22g   Fat 50g
Carbohydrate . . .60g   Saturates 20g

25 MINS   35 MINS

SERVES 4

I N G R E D I E N T S

1 kg/2 lb 4 oz potatoes

4 tbsp milk

60 g/2 oz/¼ cup butter or margarine

2 leeks, finely chopped

1 onion, finely chopped

175 g/6 oz/1½ cups grated mature (sharp)
   Cheddar cheese

1 tbsp chopped parsley or chives

1 egg, beaten

2 tbsp water

90 g/3 oz/1½ cups fresh white or
   brown breadcrumbs

vegetable oil, for shallow frying

salt and pepper

fresh flat leaf parsley sprigs, to garnish

mixed salad (greens), to serve

1 Cook the potatoes in lightly salted boiling water until tender. Drain and mash them with the milk and the butter or margarine.

2 Cook the leeks and onion in a small quantity of lightly salted boiling water for about 10 minutes until tender. Drain well.

3 In a large mixing bowl, combine the leeks and onion with the mashed potato, cheese and parsley or chives. Season to taste with salt and pepper.

4 Beat together the egg and water in a shallow bowl. Sprinkle the breadcrumbs into a separate shallow bowl. Shape the potato mixture into 12 even-sized cakes, brushing each with the egg mixture, then coating all over with the breadcrumbs.

5 Heat the oil in a large frying pan (skillet). Add the potato cakes, in batches if necessary, and fry over a low heat for about 2–3 minutes on each side, until light golden brown. Garnish with flat leaf parsley and serve with a mixed salad (greens).

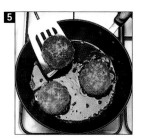

Potato & Cheese Soufflé

This soufflé is very simple to make, yet it has a delicious flavour and melts in the mouth. Choose three alternative cheeses, if preferred.

NUTRITIONAL INFORMATION

Calories ......447 Sugars 1g
Protein ....22g Fat 23g
Carbohydrate ...41g Saturates 11g

10 MINS   55 MINS

SERVES 4

INGREDIENTS

25 g/1 oz/2 tbsp butter

2 tsp plain (all-purpose) flour

900 g/2 lb floury (mealy) potatoes

8 eggs, separated

25 g/1 oz/¼ cup grated Gruyère
   (Swiss) cheese

25 g/1 oz/¼ cup crumbled blue cheese

25 g/1 oz/¼ cup grated mature
   (sharp) Cheddar cheese

salt and pepper

1 Butter a 2.4 litre/4 pint/10 cup soufflé dish and dust with the flour. Set aside.

2 Cook the potatoes in a saucepan of boiling water until tender. Mash until very smooth and then transfer to a mixing bowl to cool.

3 Beat the egg yolks into the potato and stir in the Gruyère (Swiss) cheese, blue cheese and Cheddar, mixing well. Season to taste with salt and pepper.

4 Whisk the egg whites until standing in peaks, then gently fold them into the potato mixture with a metal spoon until fully incorporated.

5 Spoon the potato mixture into the prepared soufflé dish.

6 Cook in a preheated oven, 220°C/ 425°F/Gas Mark 7, for 35–40 minutes, until risen and set. Serve immediately.

COOK'S TIP

Insert a fine skewer into the centre of the soufflé; it should come out clean when the soufflé is fully cooked through.

Potato-Topped Lentil Bake

A wonderful mixture of red lentils, tofu (bean curd) and vegetables is cooked beneath a crunchy potato topping for a really hearty meal.

NUTRITIONAL INFORMATION

Calories	627	Sugars	.........7g
Protein	........26g	Fat	..........30g
Carbohydrate	...66g	Saturates	......13g

  10 MINS   1½ HOURS

SERVES 4

INGREDIENTS

TOPPING

675 g/1½ lb floury (mealy) potatoes, diced

25 g/1 oz/2 tbsp butter

1 tbsp milk

50 g/1¾ oz/½ cup chopped pecan nuts

2 tbsp chopped thyme

thyme sprigs, to garnish

FILLING

225 g/8 oz/1 cup red lentils

60 g/2 oz/½ cup butter

1 leek, sliced

2 garlic cloves, crushed

1 celery stick, chopped

125 g/4½ oz broccoli florets

175 g/6 oz smoked tofu (bean curd), cubed

2 tsp tomato purée (paste)

salt and pepper

VARIATION

You can use almost any combination of your favourite vegetables in this dish.

1 To make the topping, cook the potatoes in a saucepan of boiling water for 10–15 minutes, or until cooked through. Drain well, add the butter and milk and mash thoroughly. Stir in the pecan nuts and chopped thyme and set aside.

2 Cook the lentils in boiling water for 20–30 minutes, or until tender. Drain and set aside.

3 Melt the butter in a frying pan (skillet). Add the leek, garlic, celery and broccoli. Fry over a medium heat, stirring frequently, for 5 minutes, until softened. Add the tofu (bean curd) cubes. Stir in the lentils, together with the tomato purée (paste). Season with salt and pepper to taste, then turn the mixture into the base of a shallow ovenproof dish.

4 Spoon the mashed potato on top of the lentil mixture, spreading to cover it completely.

5 Cook in a preheated oven, 200°C/400°F/Gas Mark 6, for about 30–35 minutes, or until the topping is golden. Garnish with sprigs of fresh thyme and serve hot.

Potato-Topped Vegetables

This is a very colourful and nutritious dish, packed full of crunchy vegetables in a tasty white wine sauce.

NUTRITIONAL INFORMATION

Calories 413	Sugars 11g
Protein 19g	Fat 18g
Carbohydrate . . .41g	Saturates 11g

🥔 20 MINS   🕐 1¼ HOURS

SERVES 4

INGREDIENTS

1 carrot, diced

175 g/6 oz cauliflower florets

175 g/6 oz broccoli florets

1 fennel bulb, sliced

75 g/2¾ oz green beans, halved

25 g/1 oz/2 tbsp butter

25 g/1 oz/¼ cup plain (all-purpose) flour

150 ml/¼ pint/⅔ cup vegetable stock

150 ml/¼ pint/⅔ cup dry white wine

150 ml/¼ pint/⅔ cup milk

175 g/6 oz chestnut (crimini)
  mushrooms, quartered

2 tbsp chopped sage

TOPPING

4 floury (mealy) potatoes, diced

25 g/1 oz/2 tbsp butter

4 tbsp natural (unsweetened) yogurt

4 tbsp grated Parmesan cheese

1 tsp fennel seeds

salt and pepper

1 Cook the carrot, cauliflower, broccoli, fennel and beans in a large saucepan of boiling water for 10 minutes, until just tender. Drain the vegetables thoroughly and set aside.

2 Melt the butter in a saucepan. Stir in the flour and cook for 1 minute. Remove from the heat and stir in the stock, wine and milk. Return to the heat and bring to the boil, stirring until thickened. Stir in the reserved vegetables, mushrooms and sage.

3 Meanwhile, make the topping. Cook the diced potatoes in a pan of boiling water for 10-15 minutes. Drain and mash with the butter, yogurt and half the cheese. Stir in the fennel seeds.

4 Spoon the vegetable mixture into a 1 litre/1¾ pint/4 cup pie dish. Spoon the potato over the top and sprinkle with the remaining cheese. Cook in a preheated oven, 190°C/375°F/Gas Mark 5, for 30–35 minutes, or until golden. Serve hot.

Jacket Potatoes with Beans

Baked jacket potatoes, topped with a tasty mixture of beans in a spicy sauce, provide a deliciously filling, high-fibre dish.

NUTRITIONAL INFORMATION

Calories 378	Sugars 9g
Protein 15g	Fat 9g
Carbohydrate . . .64g	Saturates 1g

 15 MINS   1¼ HOURS

SERVES 6

I N G R E D I E N T S

6 large potatoes

4 tbsp vegetable ghee or oil

1 large onion, chopped

2 garlic cloves, crushed

1 tsp ground turmeric

1 tbsp cumin seeds

2 tbsp mild or medium curry paste

350 g/12 oz cherry tomatoes

400 g/14 oz can black-eye beans (peas),
    drained and rinsed

400 g/14 oz can red kidney beans,
    drained and rinsed

1 tbsp lemon juice

2 tbsp tomato purée (paste)

150 ml/¼ pint/ ⅔ cup water

2 tbsp chopped fresh mint or coriander
    (cilantro)

salt and pepper

VARIATION

Instead of cutting the potatoes in half, cut a cross in each and squeeze gently to open out. Spoon some of the prepared filling into the cross and place any remaining filling to the side.

1 Scrub the potatoes and prick several times with a fork. Place in a preheated oven, 180°C/350°F/Gas Mark 4, and cook for 1–1¼ hours, or until the potatoes feel soft when gently squeezed.

2 About 20 minutes before the end of cooking time, prepare the topping. Heat the ghee or oil in a saucepan, add the onion and cook over a low heat, stirring frequently, for 5 minutes. Add the garlic, turmeric, cumin seeds and curry paste and cook gently for 1 minute.

3 Stir in the tomatoes, black-eye beans (peas) and red kidney beans, lemon juice, tomato purée (paste), water and chopped mint. Season to taste with salt and pepper, then cover and simmer over a low heat, stirring frequently, for 10 minutes.

4 When the potatoes are cooked, cut them in half and mash the flesh lightly with a fork. Spoon the prepared bean mixture on top, place on warming serving plates and serve immediately.

Spicy Potato & Nut Terrine

This delicious baked terrine has a base of mashed potato which is flavoured with nuts, cheese, herbs and spices.

NUTRITIONAL INFORMATION

Calories ....1100 Sugars 13g
Protein ....34g   Fat 93g
Carbohydrate ...31g   Saturates 22g

15 MINS   1½ HOURS

SERVES 4

INGREDIENTS

225 g/8 oz floury (mealy) potatoes, diced

225 g/8 oz pecan nuts

225 g/8 oz unsalted cashew nuts

1 onion, finely chopped

2 garlic cloves, crushed

125 g/4½ oz/1½ cups diced open-
    cap mushrooms

25 g/1 oz/2 tbsp butter

2 tbsp chopped mixed herbs

1 tsp paprika

1 tsp ground cumin

1 tsp ground coriander

4 eggs, beaten

125 g/4½ oz/½ cup full-fat soft cheese

60 g/2 oz/⅔ cup grated Parmesan cheese

salt and pepper

SAUCE

3 large tomatoes, peeled,
    seeded and chopped

2 tbsp tomato purée (paste)

75 ml/3 fl oz/⅓ cup red wine

1 tbsp red wine vinegar

pinch of caster (superfine) sugar

1 Lightly grease a 1 kg/2 lb loaf tin (pan) and line with baking parchment.

2 Cook the potatoes in a large pan of lightly salted boiling water for 10 minutes, or until cooked through. Drain and mash thoroughly.

3 Finely chop the pecan and cashew nuts or process in a food processor. Mix the nuts with the onion, garlic and mushrooms. Melt the butter in a frying pan (skillet) and cook the nut mixture for 5-7 minutes. Add the herbs and spices. Stir in the eggs, cheeses and potatoes and season to taste with salt and pepper.

4 Spoon the mixture into the prepared loaf tin (pan), pressing down firmly. Cook in a preheated oven, 190°C/375°F/Gas Mark 5, for 1 hour, or until set.

5 To make the sauce, mix the tomatoes, tomato purée (paste), wine, wine vinegar and sugar in a pan and bring to the boil, stirring. Cook for 10 minutes, or until the tomatoes have reduced. Press the sauce through a strainer or process in a food processor for 30 seconds. Turn the terrine out of the tin (pan) on to a serving plate and cut into slices. Serve with the tomato sauce.

Baked Potatoes with Pesto

This is an easy, but very filling meal. The potatoes are baked until fluffy, then they are mixed with a tasty pesto filling and baked again.

NUTRITIONAL INFORMATION

Calories	444	Sugars	.........3g
Protein	........10g	Fat	..........28g
Carbohydrate	...40g	Saturates	......13g

10 MINS   1½ HOURS

SERVES 4

INGREDIENTS

4 baking potatoes, about 225 g/8 oz each

150 ml/¼ pint/⅔ cup double (heavy) cream

75 ml/3 fl oz/⅓ cup vegetable stock

1 tbsp lemon juice

2 garlic cloves, crushed

3 tbsp chopped basil

2 tbsp pine nuts

2 tbsp grated Parmesan cheese

salt and pepper

1 Scrub the potatoes well and prick the skins with a fork. Rub a little salt into the skins and place on a baking tray (cookie sheet).

2 Cook in a preheated oven, 190°C/375°F/Gas Mark 5, for 1 hour, or until the potatoes are cooked through and the skins are crisp.

3 Remove the potatoes from the oven and cut them in half lengthways. Using a spoon, scoop the potato flesh into a mixing bowl, leaving a thin shell of potato inside the skins. Mash the potato flesh with a fork.

4 Meanwhile, mix the cream and stock in a saucepan and simmer over a low heat for about 8-10 minutes, or until reduced by half.

5 Stir in the lemon juice, garlic and chopped basil and season to taste with salt and pepper. Stir the mixture into the mashed potato flesh, together with the pine nuts.

6 Spoon the mixture back into the potato shells and sprinkle the Parmesan cheese on top. Return the potatoes to the oven for 10 minutes, or until the cheese has browned. Serve.

VARIATION

Add full-fat soft cheese or thinly sliced mushrooms to the mashed potato flesh in step 5, if you prefer.

Filled Jacket Potatoes

Cook these potatoes conventionally, wrap them in foil and keep warm at the edge of the barbecue (grill), ready to fill with inspired mixtures.

NUTRITIONAL INFORMATION

Calories 564	Sugars 14g
Protein 21g	Fat 29g
Carbohydrate ...58g	Saturates 18g

   15 MINS 1 HR 5 MINS

SERVES 4

INGREDIENTS

4 large or 8 medium baking potatoes

paprika or chilli powder, or chopped herbs,
  to garnish

MEXICAN RELISH

225 g/8 oz can sweetcorn (corn), drained

½ red (bell) pepper, seeded and chopped

5 cm/2 inch piece of cucumber,
  finely chopped

½ tsp chilli powder

salt and pepper

CHEESE & CHIVES

125 g/4½ oz/½ cup full-fat soft cheese

125 g/4½ oz/½ cup natural fromage frais

125 g/4½ oz blue cheese, cut into cubes

1 celery stick, finely chopped

2 tsp snipped chives

celery salt and pepper

SPICY MUSHROOMS

25 g/1 oz/2 tbsp butter or margarine

225 g/8 oz button mushrooms

150 g/5½ oz/⅔ cup natural
  (unsweetened) yogurt

1 tbsp tomato purée (paste)

2 tsp mild curry powder

salt and pepper

1 Scrub the potatoes and prick them with a fork. Bake in a preheated oven, 200°C/400°F/Gas Mark 6, for about 1 hour, until just tender.

2 To make the Mexican Relish, put half the sweetcorn (corn) into a bowl. Process the remainder into a blender or food processor for 10–15 seconds, or chop and mash roughly by hand. Add the puréed corn to the corn kernels with the (bell) pepper, cucumber and chilli powder. Season to taste with salt and pepper.

3 To make the Cheese & Chives filling, mix the soft cheese and fromage frais together until smooth. Add the blue cheese, celery and chives. Season with celery salt and pepper.

4 To make the Spicy Mushrooms, melt the butter or margarine in a small frying pan (skillet). Add the mushrooms and cook gently for 3–4 minutes. Remove from the heat and stir in the yogurt, tomato purée (paste) and curry powder. Season to taste with salt and pepper.

5 Wrap the cooked potatoes in foil and keep warm at the edge of the barbecue. Serve the fillings sprinkled with paprika or chilli powder or herbs.

Italian Potato Wedges

These oven-cooked potato wedges use classic pizza ingredients and are delicious served with plain meats, such as pork or lamb.

NUTRITIONAL INFORMATION

Calories	115	Sugars	.........4g
Protein	.........6g	Fat	..........5g
Carbohydrate	...13g	Saturates	.......3g

  15 MINS   35 MINS

SERVES 4

INGREDIENTS

2 large waxy potatoes, unpeeled

4 large ripe tomatoes, peeled and seeded

150 ml/ ¼ pint/⅔ cup vegetable stock

2 tbsp tomato purée (paste)

1 small yellow (bell) pepper, cut into strips

125 g/4 ½ oz button mushrooms, quartered

1 tbsp chopped fresh basil

50 g/1 ¾ oz cheese, grated

salt and pepper

1 Cut each of the potatoes into 8 equal wedges. Parboil the potatoes in a pan of boiling water for 15 minutes. Drain well and place in a shallow ovenproof dish.

2 Chop the tomatoes and add to the dish. Mix together the vegetable stock and tomato purée (paste), then pour the mixture over the potatoes and tomatoes.

3 Add the yellow (bell) pepper strips, quartered mushrooms and chopped basil. Season well with salt and pepper.

4 Sprinkle the grated cheese over the top and cook in a preheated oven, 190°C/375°F/Gas Mark 5, for 15-20 minutes until the topping is golden brown. Serve at once.

Gnocchi with Herb Sauce

These little potato dumplings are a traditional Italian appetizer but, served with a salad and bread, they make a substantial main course.

NUTRITIONAL INFORMATION

Calories 619   Sugars 3g
Protein . . . . .11g   Fat 30g
Carbohydrate . . .81g   Saturates 9g

🥔 30 MINS   🕐 30 MINS

SERVES 6

I N G R E D I E N T S

1 kg/2 lb 4 oz old potatoes, cut into
   1 cm/½ inch pieces

60 g/2 oz/¼ cup butter or margarine

1 egg, beaten

300 g/10½ oz/2½ cups plain
   (all-purpose) flour

salt

S A U C E

125 ml/4 fl oz/½ cup olive oil

2 garlic cloves, very finely chopped

1 tbsp chopped fresh oregano

1 tbsp chopped fresh basil

salt and pepper

T O   S E R V E

freshly grated Parmesan (optional)

mixed salad (greens)

warm ciabatta

1 Cook the potatoes in a saucepan of boiling salted water for about 10 minutes or until tender. Drain well.

2 Press the hot potatoes through a sieve (strainer) into a large bowl. Add 1 teaspoon of salt, the butter or margarine, egg and 150 g/5½ oz/1¼ cups of the flour. Mix well to bind together.

3 Turn on to a lightly floured surface and knead, gradually adding the remaining flour, until a smooth, soft, slightly sticky dough is formed.

4 Flour the hands and roll the dough into 2 cm/¾ inch thick rolls. Cut into 1 cm/½ inch pieces. Press the top of each piece with the floured prongs of a fork and spread out on a floured tea towel (dish cloth).

5 Bring a large saucepan of salted water to a simmer. Add the gnocchi and cook in batches for 2–3 minutes or until they rise to the surface.

6 Remove the gnocchi with a perforated spoon and put in a warmed, greased serving dish. Cover and keep warm.

7 To make the sauce, put the oil, garlic and seasoning in a pan and cook, stirring, for 3–4 minutes until the garlic is golden. Remove from the heat and stir in the herbs. Pour over the gnocchi and serve, sprinkled with Parmesan, and accompanied by salad and warm ciabatta.

Spinach Gnocchi

These gnocchi, or small dumplings, are made with potato and flavoured with spinach and nutmeg and served in a tomato and basil sauce.

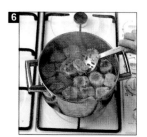

NUTRITIONAL INFORMATION

Calories	337	Sugars	.........4g
Protein	.........9g	Fat	..........10g
Carbohydrate	...52g	Saturates	.......4g

  25 MINS 🕐 1 HOUR

SERVES 4

I N G R E D I E N T S

450 g/1 lb baking potatoes

75 g/2¾ oz spinach

1 tsp water

25 g/1 oz/3 tbsp butter or margarine

1 small egg, beaten

150 g/5½ oz/¾ cup plain (all-purpose) flour

fresh basil sprigs, to garnish

T O M A T O   S A U C E

1 tbsp olive oil

1 shallot, chopped

1 tbsp tomato purée (paste)

225 g/8 oz can chopped tomatoes

2 tbsp chopped basil

85 ml/3 fl oz/6 tbsp red wine

1 tsp caster (superfine) sugar

salt and pepper

1 Cook the potatoes in their skins in a pan of boiling salted water for 20 minutes. Drain well and press through a sieve into a bowl.

2 Cook the spinach in 1 teaspoon of water for 5 minutes or until wilted. Drain and pat dry with paper towels. Chop and stir into the potatoes.

3 Add the butter or margarine, egg and half of the flour to the spinach mixture, mixing well. Turn out on to a floured surface, gradually kneading in the remaining flour to form a soft dough.

4 With floured hands, roll the dough into thin ropes and cut off 2 cm/¾ inch pieces. Press the centre of each dumpling with your finger, drawing it towards you to curl the sides of the gnocchi. Cover the gnocchi and leave to chill.

5 Heat the oil for the sauce in a pan and sauté the chopped shallots for 5 minutes. Add the tomato purée (paste), tomatoes, basil, red wine and sugar and season well. Bring to the boil and then simmer for 20 minutes.

6 Bring a pan of salted water to the boil and cook the gnocchi for 2–3 minutes or until they rise to the top of the pan. Drain well and transfer to serving dishes. Spoon the tomato sauce over the gnocchi. Garnish and serve.

Gnocchi & Tomato Sauce

Freshly made potato gnocchi are delicious, especially when they are topped with a fragrant tomato sauce.

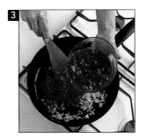

NUTRITIONAL INFORMATION

Calories 216	Sugars 5g	
Protein 5g	Fat 6g	
Carbohydrate ...39g	Saturates 1g	

30 MINS 45 MINS

SERVES 4

INGREDIENTS

350 g/12 oz floury (mealy) potatoes (those suitable for baking or mashing), halved

75 g/2¾ oz self-raising flour, plus extra for rolling out

2 tsp dried oregano

2 tbsp oil

1 large onion, chopped

2 garlic cloves, chopped

400 g/14 oz can chopped tomatoes

½ vegetable stock cube dissolved in 100 ml/3½ fl oz/⅓ cup boiling water

2 tbsp basil, shredded, plus whole leaves to garnish

salt and pepper

Parmesan cheese, grated, to serve

1 Bring a large saucepan of water to the boil. Add the potatoes and cook for 12–15 minutes or until tender. Drain and leave to cool.

2 Peel and then mash the potatoes with the salt and pepper, sifted flour and oregano. Mix together with your hands to form a dough.

3 Heat the oil in a pan. Add the onions and garlic and cook for 3–4 minutes.

Add the tomatoes and stock and cook, uncovered, for 10 minutes. Season with salt and pepper to taste.

4 Roll the potato dough into a sausage about 2.5 cm/1 inch in diameter. Cut the sausage into 2.5 cm/1 inch lengths. Flour your hands, then press a fork into each piece to create a series of ridges on one side and the indent of your index finger on the other.

5 Bring a large saucepan of water to the boil and cook the gnocchi, in batches, for 2–3 minutes. They should rise to the surface when cooked. Drain well and keep warm.

6 Stir the basil into the tomato sauce and pour over the gnocchi. Garnish with basil leaves and season with pepper to taste. Sprinkle with Parmesan and serve at once.

VARIATION

Try serving the gnocchi with Pesto Sauce for a change.

Potato & Spinach Gnocchi

These small potato dumplings are flavoured with spinach, cooked in boiling water and served with a simple tomato sauce.

NUTRITIONAL INFORMATION

Calories	.315	Sugars	.7g
Protein	.8g	Fat	.8g
Carbohydrate	.56g	Saturates	.1g

 20 MINS   30 MINS

SERVES 4

I N G R E D I E N T S

300 g/10½ oz floury (mealy) potatoes, diced

175 g/6 oz spinach

1 egg yolk

1 tsp olive oil

125 g/4½ oz/1 cup plain (all-purpose) flour

salt and pepper

spinach leaves, to garnish

S A U C E

1 tbsp olive oil

2 shallots, chopped

1 garlic clove, crushed

300 ml/½ pint/1¼ cups passata (sieved tomatoes)

2 tsp soft light brown sugar

1 Cook the diced potatoes in a saucepan of boiling water for 10 minutes or until cooked through. Drain and mash the potatoes.

2 Meanwhile, in a separate pan, blanch the spinach in a little boiling water for 1-2 minutes. Drain the spinach and shred the leaves.

3 Transfer the mashed potato to a lightly floured chopping board and make a well in the centre. Add the egg yolk, olive oil, spinach and a little of the flour and quickly mix the ingredients into the potato, adding more flour as you go, until you have a firm dough. Divide the mixture into very small dumplings.

4 Cook the gnocchi, in batches, in a saucepan of boiling salted water for about 5 minutes or until they rise to the surface.

5 Meanwhile, make the sauce. Put the oil, shallots, garlic, passata (sieved tomatoes) and sugar into a saucepan and cook over a low heat for 10-15 minutes or until the sauce has thickened.

6 Drain the gnocchi using a perforated spoon and transfer to warm serving dishes. Spoon the sauce over the gnocchi and garnish with the fresh spinach leaves.

VARIATION

Add chopped fresh herbs and cheese to the gnocchi dough instead of the spinach, if you prefer.

Potato Noodles

Potatoes are used to make a 'pasta' dough which is cut into thin noodles and boiled. The noodles are served with a bacon and mushroom sauce.

NUTRITIONAL INFORMATION

Calories 810   Sugars 5g
Protein . . . . .21g   Fat 47g
Carbohydrate . . .81g   Saturates 26g

 30 MINS   25 MINS

SERVES 4

INGREDIENTS

450 g/1 lb floury (mealy) potatoes, diced

225 g/8 oz/2 cups plain (all-purpose) flour

1 egg, beaten

1 tbsp milk

salt and pepper

parsley sprig, to garnish

SAUCE

1 tbsp vegetable oil

1 onion, chopped

1 garlic clove, crushed

125 g/4½ oz open-capped
   mushrooms, sliced

3 smoked bacon slices, chopped

50 g/1¾ oz Parmesan cheese, grated

300 ml/½ pint/1¼ cups double
   (heavy) cream

2 tbsp chopped fresh parsley

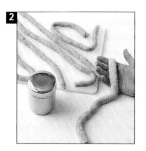

1 Cook the diced potatoes in a saucepan of boiling water for 10 minutes or until cooked through. Drain well. Mash the potatoes until smooth, then beat in the flour, egg and milk. Season with salt and pepper to taste and bring together to form a stiff paste.

2 On a lightly floured surface, roll out the paste to form a thin sausage shape. Cut the sausage into 2.5 cm/1 inch lengths. Bring a large pan of salted water to the boil, drop in the dough pieces and cook for 3-4 minutes. They will rise to the surface when cooked.

3 To make the sauce, heat the oil in a pan and sauté the onion and garlic for 2 minutes. Add the mushrooms and bacon and cook for 5 minutes. Stir in the cheese, cream and parsley, and season.

4 Drain the noodles and transfer to a warm pasta bowl. Spoon the sauce over the top and toss to mix. Garnish with a parsley sprig and serve.

COOK'S TIP

Make the dough in advance, then wrap and store the noodles in the refrigerator for up to 24 hours.

Shepherd's Pie

Minced (ground) lamb or beef cooked with onions, carrots, herbs and tomatoes and with a topping of piped creamed potatoes.

NUTRITIONAL INFORMATION

Calories ....378 Sugars 8g
Protein ....33g Fat 12g
Carbohydrate ...37g Saturates 4g

10 MINS   1½ HOURS

SERVES 4–5

I N G R E D I E N T S

700 g/1 lb 9 oz lean minced (ground) or
  lamb or beef

2 onions, chopped

225 g/8 oz carrots, diced

1–2 garlic cloves, crushed

1 tbsp plain (all-purpose) flour

200 ml/7 fl oz/scant 1 cup beef stock

200 g/7 oz can chopped tomatoes

1 tsp Worcestershire sauce

1 tsp chopped fresh sage or oregano or
  ½ tsp dried sage or oregano

750 g–1 kg/1½–2 lb potatoes

25 g/1 oz/2 tbsp margarine

3–4 tbsp skimmed milk

125 g/4½ oz button mushrooms, sliced
  (optional)

salt and pepper

1 Place the meat in a heavy-based saucepan with no extra fat and cook gently, stirring frequently, until the meat begins to brown.

2 Add the onions, carrots and garlic and continue to cook gently for about 10 minutes. Stir in the flour and cook for a minute or so, then gradually stir in the stock and tomatoes and bring to the boil.

3 Add the Worcestershire sauce, seasoning and herbs, cover the pan and simmer gently for about 25 minutes, giving an occasional stir.

4 Cook the potatoes in boiling salted water until tender, then drain thoroughly and mash, beating in the margarine, seasoning and sufficient milk to give a piping consistency. Place in a piping bag fitted with a large star nozzle (tip).

5 Stir the mushrooms (if using) into the meat and adjust the seasoning. Turn into a shallow ovenproof dish.

6 Pipe the potatoes evenly over the meat. Cook in a preheated oven at 200°C/400°F/Gas Mark 6 for about 30 minutes until piping hot and the potatoes are golden brown.

VARIATION

If liked, a mixture of boiled potatoes and parsnips or swede may be used for the topping.

Lamb & Potato Masala

To create delicious Indian dishes at home – simply open a can of curry sauce, add a few interesting ingredients and you have a splendid meal.

NUTRITIONAL INFORMATION

Calories 513   Sugars 6g
Protein . . . . .40g   Fat 27g
Carbohydrate . . .30g   Saturates 8g

 15 MINS   1½ HOURS

SERVES 4

I N G R E D I E N T S

750 g/1 lb 10 oz lean lamb (from the leg)

3 tbsp ghee or vegetable oil

500 g/1 lb 2 oz potatoes, peeled and cut in large 2.5 cm/1 inch pieces

1 large onion, peeled, quartered and sliced

2 garlic cloves, peeled and crushed

175 g/6 oz mushrooms, thickly sliced

1 x 283 g/10 oz can Tikka Masala Curry Sauce

300 ml/½ pint/1¼ cups water

salt

3 tomatoes, halved and cut into thin slices

125g/4½ oz spinach, washed and stalks trimmed

sprigs of mint, to garnish

COOK'S TIP

Spinach leaves wilt quickly during cooking, so if the leaves are young and tender add them whole to the mixture; larger leaves may be coarsely shredded, if wished, before adding to the pan.

1 Cut the lamb into 2.5 cm/1 inch cubes. Heat the ghee or oil in a large pan, add the lamb and fry over moderate heat for 3 minutes or until sealed all over. Removethe lamb from the pan.

2 Add the potatoes, onion, garlic and mushrooms and fry for 3-4 minutes, stirring frequently.

3 Stir the curry sauce and water into the pan, add the lamb, mix well and season with salt to taste. Cover and cook very gently for 1 hour or until the lamb is tender and cooked through, stirring occasionally.

4 Add the sliced tomatoes and the spinach to the pan, pushing the leaves well down into the mixture, then cover and cook for a further 10 minutes until the spinach is cooked and tender.

5 Garnish with mint sprigs and serve hot.

Beef & Tomato Gratin

A satisfying bake of lean minced beef, courgettes (zucchini) and tomatoes cooked in a low-fat 'custard' with a cheesy crust.

NUTRITIONAL INFORMATION

Calories ....278 Sugars 10g
Protein ....29g Fat 10g
Carbohydrate ...20g Saturates 5g

10 MINS   1¼ HOURS

SERVES 4

INGREDIENTS

350 g/12 oz lean beef, minced (ground)

1 large onion, finely chopped

1 tsp dried mixed herbs

1 tbsp plain (all-purpose) flour

300 ml/½ pint/1¼ cups beef stock

1 tbsp tomato purée (paste)

2 large tomatoes, thinly sliced

4 medium courgettes (zucchini), thinly sliced

2 tbsp cornflour (cornstarch)

300 ml/½ pint/1¼ cups skimmed milk

150 ml/5 fl oz/⅔ cup low-fat natural fromage frais (unsweetened yogurt)

1 medium egg yolk

4 tbsp Parmesan cheese, freshly grated

salt and pepper

TO SERVE

crusty bread

steamed vegetables

1 Preheat the oven to 190°C/375°F/Gas Mark 5. In a large frying pan (skillet), dry-fry the beef and onion for 4–5 minutes until browned.

2 Stir in the dried mixed herbs, flour, beef stock and tomato purée (paste), and season. Bring to the boil and simmer for 30 minutes until the mixture has thickened.

3 Transfer the beef mixture to an ovenproof gratin dish. Cover with a layer of the sliced tomatoes and then add a layer of sliced courgettes (zucchini). Blend the cornflour (cornstarch) with a little milk. Pour the remaining milk into a saucepan and bring to the boil. Add the cornflour (cornstarch) mixture and cook, stirring, for 1–2 minutes until thickened. Remove from the heat and beat in the fromage frais (yogurt) and egg yolk. Season well.

4 Spread the white sauce over the layer of courgettes (zucchini). Place the dish on to a baking sheet and sprinkle with grated Parmesan. Bake in the oven for 25–30 minutes until golden-brown. Serve with crusty bread and vegetables.

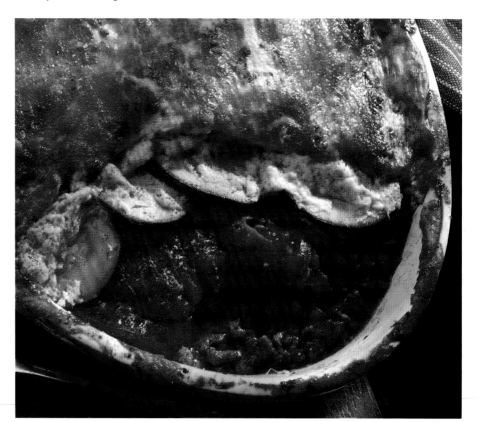

Chicken & Potato Bake

Make this when new potatoes are in season. A medium onion or a few shallots can be substituted for the spring onions (scallions).

NUTRITIONAL INFORMATION

Calories 323	Sugars 9g	
Protein 30g	Fat 10g	
Carbohydrate . . .29g	Saturates 2g	

 10 MINS   1¼ HOURS

SERVES 4

I N G R E D I E N T S

2 tbsp olive oil

4 lean chicken breasts

1 bunch spring onions (scallions), trimmed and chopped

350 g/12 oz young spring carrots, scrubbed and sliced

125 g/4½ oz dwarf green beans, trimmed and sliced

600 ml/1 pint/2½ cups chicken stock

350 g/12 oz small new potatoes, scrubbed

1 small bunch mixed fresh herbs, such as thyme, rosemary, bay and parsley

salt and pepper

2 tbsp cornflour (cornstarch)

2–3 tbsp cold water

sprigs of fresh mixed herbs, to garnish

1 Heat the oil in a large flameproof casserole and add the chicken breasts. Gently fry for 5-8 minutes until browned on both sides. Lift from the casserole with a perforated spoon and set aside.

2 Add the spring onions (scallions), carrots and green beans and gently fry for 3-4 minutes.

3 Return the chicken to the casserole and pour in the stock. Add the potatoes and herbs. Season, bring to the boil, then cover the casserole and transfer to the oven. Bake in a preheated oven at 190°C/375°F/Gas Mark 5 for 40-50 minutes until the potatoes are tender.

4 Blend the cornflour (cornstarch) with the cold water. Add to the casserole, stirring until blended and thickened. Cover and cook for a further 5 minutes. Garnish with fresh herbs and serve.

COOK'S TIP

Use your favourite combination of herbs for this dish. If fresh herbs are unavailable, use half the quantity of dried mixed herbs. Alternatively, use a bouquet garni sachet which is usually a combination of bay, thyme and parsley.

Baked Potatoes with Salsa

This is a great way to eat a baked potato! Once cooked, the flesh is flavoured with avocado and served with a hot tomato salsa.

NUTRITIONAL INFORMATION

Calories 274	Sugars 4g
Protein 10g	Fat 8g
Carbohydrate ...43g	Saturates 2g

15 MINS   1 HOUR

SERVES 4

I N G R E D I E N T S

4 baking potatoes, about 225 g/8 oz each

1 large ripe avocado

1 tsp lemon juice

175 g/6 oz smoked tofu (bean curd), diced

2 garlic cloves, crushed

1 onion, chopped finely

1 tomato, chopped finely

125 g/4½ oz mixed salad leaves

fresh coriander (cilantro) sprigs, to garnish

S A L S A

2 ripe tomatoes, seeded and diced

1 tbsp chopped coriander (cilantro)

1 shallot, diced finely

1 green chilli, diced

1 tbsp lemon juice

salt and pepper

1 Scrub the potatoes and prick the skins with a fork. Rub a little salt into the skins and place them on a baking tray (cookie sheet).

2 Cook in a preheated oven, 190°C/ 375°F/Gas Mark 5, for 1 hour or until cooked through and the skins are crisp.

3 Cut the potatoes in half lengthways and scoop the flesh into a bowl, leaving a thin layer of potato inside the shells.

4 Halve and stone the avocado. Using a spoon, scoop out the avocado flesh and add to the bowl containing the potato. Stir in the lemon juice and mash the mixture together with a fork. Mix in the tofu (bean curd), garlic, onion and tomato. Spoon the mixture into one half of the potato shells.

5 Arrange the mixed salad leaves on top of the guacamole mixture and place the other half of the potato shell on top.

6 To make the salsa, mix the tomatoes, coriander (cilantro), shallots, chilli, lemon juice and salt and pepper to taste in a bowl. Garnish the potatoes with sprigs of fresh coriander (cilantro) and serve with the salsa.

Potato Muffins

These light-textured muffins rise like little soufflés in the oven and are best eaten warm. The dried fruits can be varied according to taste.

NUTRITIONAL INFORMATION

Calories	98	Sugars	.......11g
Protein	.........3g	Fat	..........2g
Carbohydrate	...18g	Saturates	.....0.5g

 20 MINS   35 MINS

MAKES 12

INGREDIENTS

175 g/6 oz floury (mealy) potatoes, diced

75 g/2¾ oz/¾ cup self-raising (self-rising) flour

2 tbsp soft light brown sugar

1 tsp baking powder

125 g/4½ oz/¾ cup raisins

4 eggs, separated

1 Lightly grease and flour 12 muffin tins (pans).

2 Cook the diced potatoes in a saucepan of boiling water for 10 minutes, or until tender. Drain well and mash until completely smooth.

3 Transfer the mashed potatoes to a mixing bowl and add the flour, sugar, baking powder, raisins and egg yolks. Stir well to mix thoroughly.

4 In a clean bowl, whisk the egg whites until standing in peaks. Using a metal spoon, gently fold them into the potato mixture until fully incorporated.

5 Divide the mixture between the prepared tins (pans).

6 Cook in a preheated oven, 200°C/400°F/Gas Mark 6, for 10 minutes. Reduce the oven temperature to 160°C/325°F/Gas Mark 3 and cook the muffins for a further 7–10 minutes, or until risen.

7 Remove the muffins from the tins (pans) and serve warm.

COOK'S TIP

Instead of spreading the muffins with plain butter, serve them with cinnamon butter made by blending 60 g/2 oz/½ cup butter with a large pinch of ground cinnamon.

This is a Parragon Book
This edition published in 2002

Parragon
Queen Street House
4 Queen Street
Bath BA1 1HE, UK

ISBN: 0-75257-539-2

Printed in China

NOTE

This book uses metric and imperial measurements. Follow the same units of
measurement throughout; do not mix metric and imperial. All spoon measurements
are level: teaspoons are assumed to be 5 ml and tablespoons are assumed to be 15 ml.
Unless otherwise stated, milk is assumed to be full fat, eggs and individual vegetables
such as potatoes are medium and pepper is freshly ground black pepper.

The nutritional information provided for each recipe is per serving or per person.
Optional ingredients, variations or serving suggestions have not been included in the
calculations. The times given for each recipe are an approximate guide only because
the preparation times may differ according to the techniques used by different
people and the cooking times may vary as a result of the type of oven used.

Recipes using raw or very lightly cooked eggs should be
avoided by infants, the elderly, pregnant women, convalescents
and anyone suffering from an illness.

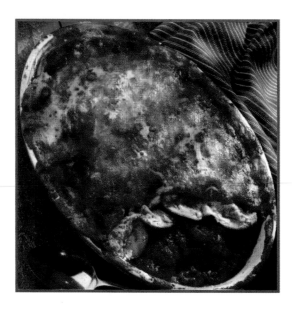